"Out of a desire for everyone to experience the depths of God's infinite love and mercy, Deacon Gerard-Marie Anthony offers rich spiritual insights and grace-filled reflections that will help you find true joy in God's loving embrace. *Peaceful Hearts, Zealous Hearts* is a life-changing spiritual journey that will leave you transformed by the tender and merciful Heart of Jesus and the Immaculate Heart of Mary. You will discover in these pages that divine mercy is a source of human flourishing and a wellspring of love that will inspire you to trust in the power of Christ's Most Sacred Heart."

—Deacon Harold Burke-Sivers,
author of *Building a Civilization of Love: A Catholic Response to Racism*

"Deacon Gerard Anthony has written a beautiful book that reveals how our good God has spoken to us and continues to speak to us through the tender Heart of His Son. The devotions to the Sacred Heart of Jesus and His Divine Mercy together reveal the unfathomable love of our Blessed Lord for His people. All who prayerfully read this wonderful book will be enabled to enter more deeply into the mystery of God's love. This work is a gift to Our Lord and His Church."

—Dr. Timothy O'Donnell,
President of Christendom College,
author of *Heart of the Redeemer,* and
presenter of *Heart of Jesus* (EWTN)

"I highly recommend this book to remind us of God's infinite and unconditional love for mankind—simply put, for you and me. In reading this book, my heart was burning with great love for God, but that love actually burst into flames, inspired by God's invitation to *love* and, in turn, my response to *His love* and *mercy*. Read and be ready to fall in love with God. Let us not wait. Our Lover (God) is waiting."

—Dr. Seggy Acosta, Stress and Pain Specialist, founder of S.T.R.E.S.S. Centre Inc., and author of *Diabolical or Psychological: The Differentiation of Psychological Diseases from Diabolical Disorders*

"An important treatise to connect Catholic devotion, divine truth, and divine mercy to the heart of Jesus Christ. In the sacrament of the Eucharist dwells the fullness of the Divinity, of sacredness, and of divine mercy. In a worldwide Eucharistic crusade, let us adore and console the Eucharistic Heart of Jesus, imploring from Him torrents of graces for the Church and the entire world."

—+ Athanasius Schneider, Auxiliary Bishop of the Archdiocese of St. Mary in Astana

"*Peaceful Hearts, Zealous Hearts* is a masterfully crafted handbook exploring the Divine Mercy and Sacred Heart devotions and serving as a beacon of hope. Emphasizing humanity's ultimate purpose in connecting with the divine, it advocates for committed prayer to unite with God, specifically within the Sacred Heart of Jesus through Divine Mercy. This concise guide offers practical insights for daily integration, acting as a valuable road map for a deeper connection with faith. The book also addresses how these devotions complement each other and can heal the vices of modernism and acedia, showcasing Deacon Anthony's passionate perspective and making it an inspiring companion for believers and seekers alike."

—Anitha George, National Coordinator, Shalom World Prayer Channel

"This work by Deacon Gerard-Marie is a masterpiece on confronting modernism. His research and his application of Consecration to the Sacred Heart and Divine Mercy make the book a must-read for those seeking to combat this heresy that is decimating our Church. Deacon Gerard offers, in holy detail, a blueprint for the sanctification of oneself and for combating head-on the cancer of modernism. I highly recommend his fantastic book for all engaged in the New Evangelization.

—Deacon Cody Miller,
Spiritual Director in the Legion of Mary

"*Peaceful Hearts, Zealous Hearts* is a precious jewel that unites two essential devotions for any Catholic seeking to advance in the spiritual life, what Our Lord calls 'the one thing necessary.' "

—Dr. Nick Lebish, ScriptureAndTradition.com

"*Peaceful Hearts, Zealous Hearts* is an easy-to-read, highly practical, and urgent reminder to all Catholics that the solution to all the problems of aching mankind lies in the very heart of the Savior, a heart that forever throbs with an infinite love and a superabundance of mercy toward all souls. Read this book and be renewed in living out these vitally important and complementary devotions to the Sacred Heart and Divine Mercy, both heavenly remedies for these troubling times."

— Fr. Jacinto Mary Chapin, F.I., Vocation Director
for the Franciscan Friars of the Immaculate

"St. Thomas Aquinas wrote, 'Contemplation of goodness is the beginning of spiritual love.' Deacon Anthony prepares the reader's heart for deeper spiritual love with this contemplative work on the Sacred Heart and Divine Mercy. With each page, the reader gains a greater knowledge of these two essential devotions. And with each page, the reader is given the opportunity to further develop a peaceful and zealous heart."

—Dr. Andrew Kubick, Deputy Director,
National Center for Religious Freedom Education

Peaceful Hearts, Zealous Hearts

Deacon Gerard-Marie Anthony

Peaceful Hearts, Zealous Hearts

How the Sacred Heart and Divine Mercy Devotions' Complementary Messages Make Us New

SOPHIA INSTITUTE PRESS
Manchester, New Hampshire

Cover design by Emma Helstrom.

Cover image: detail from an 1874 print (LC-DIG-pga-11334), Wikimedia Commons.

Interior images: *Christ showing His Sacred Heart*, by Jean Baptiste Bethune, ca. 1880, courtesy of Wikimedia Commons; Divine Mercy illustration © Mary MacArthur.

Nihil obstat: + Michael F. Burbidge, *Censor Deputatus*
Imprimatur: + Michael F. Burbidge, Bishop of Arlington,
February 12, 2024

The *nihil obstat* and *imprimatur* are an official declaration that a book, pamphlet, or prayer is free of doctrinal or moral error. No implication is contained therein that those who have granted the *nihil obstat* or *imprimatur* agree with the contents, opinions or statements expressed.

Sophia Institute Press
Box 5284, Manchester, NH 03108
1-800-888-9344
www.SophiaInstitute.com

Sophia Institute Press is a registered trademark of Sophia Institute.

paperback ISBN 979-8-88911-258-7
ebook ISBN 979-8-88911-259-4

Library of Congress Control Number: 2024932570

First printing

This book is dedicated to the following:

The Sacred Heart and Divine Mercy of Jesus:
have mercy on us, and we trust in You

Our Lady of Nazareth: through her, the Heart of Jesus
and God's Mercy became flesh and dwelt among us

St. Margaret Mary Alacoque and
St. Faustina of the Blessed Sacrament

All parishes and families in which the Sacred Heart is
enthroned and who are dedicated to the Divine Mercy

All who are looking for hope: may you find it in
the Heart of Christ through our dear Mother Mary

Contents

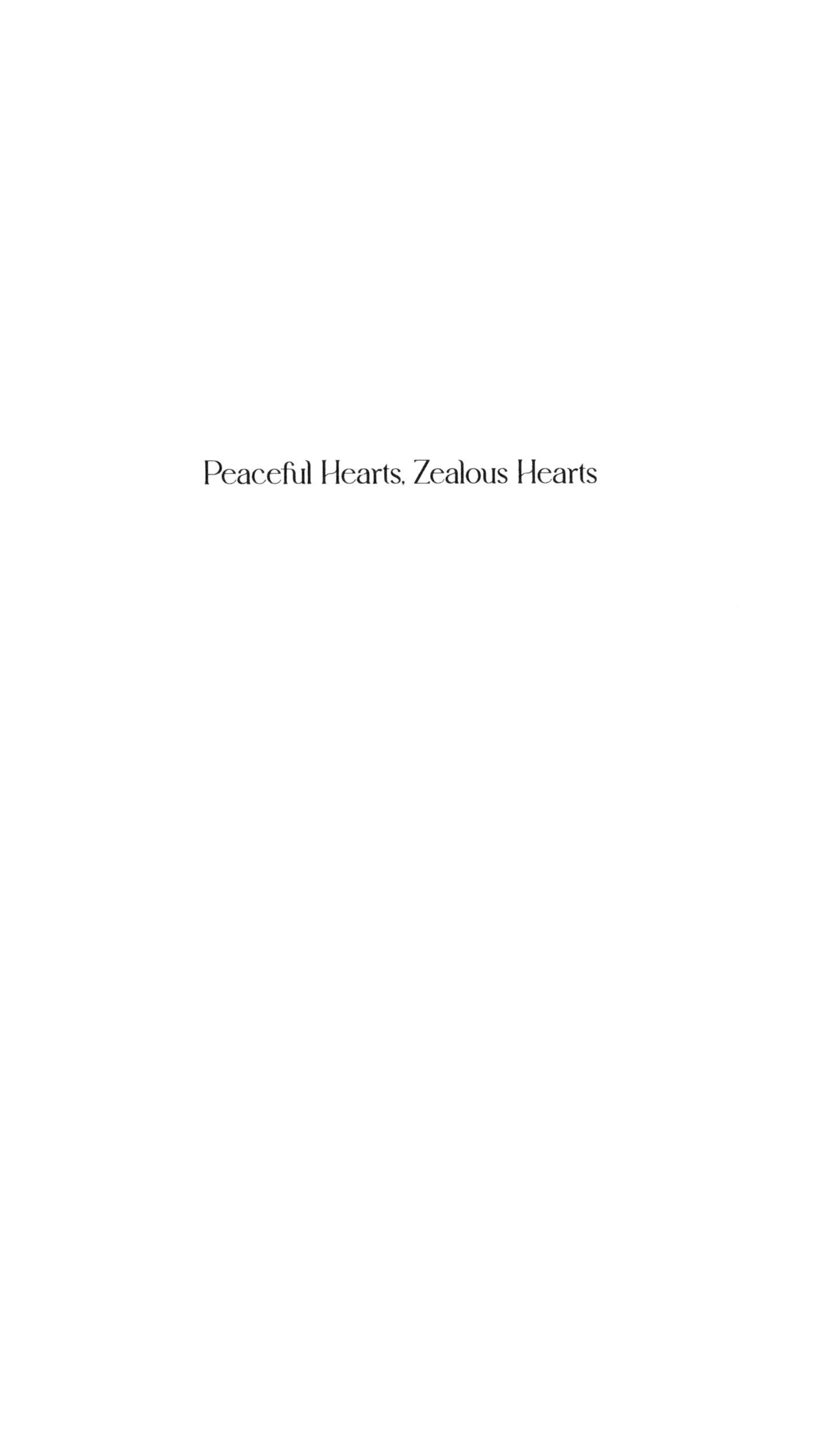

Peaceful Hearts, Zealous Hearts

Introduction

Story of the Heart

There are many experiences in life that can touch our hearts; some touch us so deeply that we remember them forever. While on a high school mission trip to Jamaica, my eyes were opened to truth, beauty, and goodness. The Jamaicans taught my classmates and me how to sing, to dance, and, more importantly, to love. I remember trying to swim through a waterfall. The Jamaicans saw that I could not make it through the waterfall, and although they had met me just a couple of days earlier, they formed a human chain and pulled me to safety! They risked their lives for me, and it left a profound impact.

But one experience changed my life forever. The Jamaicans took me to a colony for the abandoned. There I met a man with leprosy. I wanted to return the same love that was shown to me at the waterfall. The leper had lost part of his arm and some of his facial skin to the disease. Leprosy is a bacterial disease that rots away the skin, a disease that we hear about in the Bible. Leprosy can be treated today with antibiotics, though poorer countries often do not have access to these medicines. I spoke with this leper for ten minutes before our leader summoned me. Before leaving him, I told the man with leprosy, "Thank you for the wonderful time" and went to shake his hand. Tearing up, the man extended the nub that used to be his arm. I thought to myself, "What were you thinking? Here we had this great conversation, and you had to go and ruin it by offering to shake his hand—a hand that he doesn't have. Way to make him feel bad!" I began to apologize profusely as my intention was to say thank you; instead, I thought I hurt his feelings. The man said, sniffling, "That's the first time someone's taken the time to talk to me in years!" Tears were shed, and lives were changed, mine included, because we were able to speak heart-to-heart.

Cor ad Cor Loquitur

My encounter with the leper is how God wants to talk to us, heart-to-heart—*cor ad cor loquitur*. This book will begin by looking at the work of the Holy Trinity in speaking "heart-to-heart," Person-to-Person (and an additional "Person" because there are three Persons in the Trinity), to one another. This Trinitarian blueprint is the model for the Sacred Heart of Jesus and Divine Mercy devotions.

Then we will look at the scriptural origins of the Sacred Heart and Divine Mercy devotions. This quick look at these devotions will allow us to take in God's Holy Word, which in effect, communicates His heart. We will see how the Old and New Testaments, especially the Psalms, point to the communication of love between God and man—a communication that brings about consolation and inspiration.

Next, we will examine the historical roots of the Sacred Heart and Divine Mercy devotions. Understanding the historical context is important because these devotions were given to refute specific heresies that separate us from God's love.

Chapters 4 and 5 will look at what these devotions involve—specifically, five ways to live out each—and how they inspire us and affect our lives.

In the final chapters, we will see how these devotions complement each other and lead to a renewal of individual hearts, society, and the world. Let us get to work, beginning our journey with the words of the psalmist: "Create in me a clean heart, O God, and put a new and right spirit within me" (51:10).

1

The Work of God through the Heart of God

Love takes work! This profound statement is also the foundational principle of our humanity. Why? Because if someone were to reverse this sentence, he would get at the very essence of God. God is a communion of Persons, a tri-unity of Persons who work together to do liturgy. Liturgy comes from the Greek word *leitourgia*, which means "work of the people" or "work on behalf of the people." What is the work of the three Persons of the Trinity, God's liturgy, even before time began? It is love. The Father loves the Son, and the Son receives that love and returns it to the Father. That Love is not just a thing but is a Divine Person, the Holy Spirit.

So the love of God in theology (intrinsically within God) has five aspects: one God, two processions (begetting and spiration), three Persons (Father, Son, and Holy Spirit), four relations (Father-Son: paternity; Son-Father: filiation; Father and Son–Holy Spirit: spiration; Holy Spirit–Father and Son: passive spiration and procession), five notions (five properties—things that allow us to note the relations—attributed to the Divine Persons: innascibility, paternity, filiation, spiration, and procession). *Innascibility* means the property of being a source without a source, which points out the Person of the Father. The other four notions involve the relations of one Person to the other Persons in the

Trinity).[1] So we see that the work of God is essentially love, a matter of the heart, so to say.

That matter of the heart, the love of God, is poured out from the Trinity to creation. This is at the heart of God's making a covenant with mankind on the seventh day of creation (Gen. 2:1-3). A covenant happens between persons saying in binding language, "I belong to you, and you belong to me." This is exactly what the Persons in the Trinity have been doing for all eternity. God desires mankind to share in this covenantal liturgy of love. This is God's *misericordiae*. The English word *mercy* comes from this Latin word: *miser* = to have pity or take compassion; *cor* = heart.

God has compassion on man and invites him into this covenantal love, which is an act of mercy. God performs three great acts of mercy for mankind, each being attributed to a particular Person of the Trinity. Although all Persons in the Trinity take part in these acts of mercy, each act is attributed to a particular person to highlight the distinct relation or mission, as Fr. Chris Alar, M.I.C., specifies:

God the Father—Creation
God the Son—Redemption
God the Holy Spirit—Sanctification (a.k.a. "Restoration")[2]

As noted above, the Father invites us into the Trinity's love. He invites us not because we deserve it but as a free gift. This free gift in Latin is called *gratis*, which is where we get the word *grace*. So, the first grace of mercy attributed to God the Father is creation.

1 St. Thomas Aquinas, *Summa Theologiae* I, Qs. 27–43, New Advent, https://www.newadvent.org/summa/1.htm.

2 Fr. Chris Alar, M.I.C., *Understanding Divine Mercy* (Stockbridge, MA: Marian Press, 2021), 16–18.

Unfortunately, humanity separated itself from God shortly after creation. This brought mankind into a new type of relationship that did not embrace God's love. Mankind's intellect and will were darkened, and man became a slave of the devil. However, God bought back mankind, i.e., redeemed us, with the price of the precious blood of the Son. We hear this numerous times in Scripture:

> For God so loved the world that he gave his only Son, so that everyone who believes in him may not perish but may have eternal life. Indeed, God did not send the Son into the world to condemn the world, but in order that the world might be saved through him. (John 3:16–17)

> Or do you not know that your body is a temple of the Holy Spirit within you, which you have from God, and that you are not your own? For you were bought with a price; therefore glorify God in your body. (1 Cor. 6:19–20)

> You know that you were ransomed from the futile ways inherited from your ancestors, not with perishable things like silver or gold, but with the precious blood of Christ, like that of a lamb without defect or blemish. He was destined before the foundation of the world, but was revealed at the end of the ages for your sake. Through him you have come to trust in God, who raised him from the dead and gave him glory, so that your faith and hope are set on God. (1 Pet. 1:18–21)

Thus, the mercy of redemption is attributed to the Son.

The Father wanted to do more than just buy back humanity; He wanted to make us new and restore what was lost. He wanted to restore us to the covenantal liturgy in which we were made to dwell. This third work of mercy, sanctification, is attributed to the

Holy Spirit. In this, our intellects and wills are enlightened once again with the divine light, although the effects of Original Sin remain in us. This act of mercy allows the divine life to dwell in us, making us into the image of Christ the Son. Conformed in the image of Christ, we can do the work of God, which is charity. Thus, we see the work of God compassionately poured out in love upon creation. This threefold gratuitous outpouring of divine love upon humanity is called mercy.

However, this outpouring of divine love demands a response from us. This is where we see a secondary view of God's heart in Genesis:

> The LORD saw that the wickedness of humankind was great in the earth, and that every inclination of the thoughts of their hearts was only evil continually. And the LORD was sorry that he had made humankind on the earth, and it grieved him to his heart. (6:5–6)

This is the first time God's heart is mentioned in Scripture, and it speaks of man's wickedness in wounding it. The passage alludes to a need to "console the heart of God." This is a secondary *leitourgia*, or work of the people, between God and man—that of consolation.

Clearly, God loves and consoles humanity by gratuitously pouring out His love upon us through a trifold grace of mercy in creation, redemption, and sanctification. In mercy, God consoles the heart of man. At the same time, God deserves our response of love, a consolation, so to speak, in justice to Him. These come together in Jesus. As Pope St. John Paul II notes: Jesus Christ is "the human face [and heart] of God and the divine face [and heart] of man."[3]

[3] Pope John Paul II, post-synodal apostolic exhortation *Ecclesia in America* (January 22, 1999), no. 67.

Since Jesus is the eternal Word and Son of Man, in Him the divine and human meet. The Sacred Heart and Divine Mercy devotions are designed to console both God's heart and man's heart (the Mystical Body of Christ) through Him. In this, the *totus Christus*, the total Christ—both Christ as the Head and humanity as His Mystical Body, taken up into His life—is now consoled. The consolation and mercy of love were meant to be united in the plan of God "through Jesus, in Jesus, and for Jesus" (see Rom. 11:36), as we say in the Doxology in every Mass, for all eternity. To understand this unity, let us dive deeper into Scripture.

2

The Heart of God in Scripture

We know that "all scripture is inspired by God and is useful for teaching, for reproof, for correction, and for training in righteousness, so that everyone who belongs to God may be proficient, equipped for every good work" (2 Tim. 3:16–17). Therefore, looking at the Sacred Heart and Divine Mercy devotions through their scriptural foundations will deepen their meaning for us and increase their effectiveness in our lives. Specifically, we will see a beautiful tapestry depicting the work and heart of God woven throughout Scripture.

Let us start with devotion to the Sacred Heart.[4] Here, we go back to the seventh day of creation in Genesis:

> And on the seventh day God finished the work that he had done, and he rested on the seventh day from all the work that he had done. So God blessed the seventh day and hallowed it, because on it God rested from all the work that he had done in creation. (2:2–3)

It was on the seventh day that God rested. Where did He rest? He rested not in the sun and moon or in the plants, fish, or beasts but

[4] For a more in-depth study of the Sacred Heart, I recommend Dr. Timothy O'Donnell's book *Heart of the Redeemer: An Apologia for the Contemporary and Perennial Value of the Devotion to the Sacred Heart of Jesus* (San Francisco: Ignatius Press, 1992).

in man and woman. In order to understand this, we must properly understand what is meant by *rest* and then look at the reason for God's resting in man and woman.

This rest does not mean that God took a holy nap. If He did "rest" in this sense because He was tired, all of creation would have ceased to exist, since He holds all things in existence. We see this in the Letter to the Colossians, when St. Paul speaks of Jesus:

> He is the image of the invisible God, the firstborn of all creation; for in him all things in heaven and on earth were created, things visible and invisible, whether thrones or dominions or rulers or powers—all things have been created through him and for him. *He himself is before all things, and in him all things hold together*. (1:15–17, emphasis mine)

So God does not rest as we think of resting . We must look at the difference between work and rest to understand the meaning of God's rest. When you work, most of the time you are trying to complete a task, which is the objective meaning of work. However, work is not just about completing tasks; it can also be an act of love (doing something for someone–love of neighbor—and being enriched personally by it—love of self). Work can be personal; it can touch hearts (both others' and our own), which is the subjective sense of work. Genesis 2 proclaims that when you insert love into work, it becomes not just a task but a time of refreshment. Work connects people together, heart-to-heart, through love. This was the work of the seventh-day covenant. It connected God and man: *cor ad cor loquitur*. Man was to rest in God, have devotion to Him; and God, in return, would rest in humanity. This would be what made man complete, truly beautiful. In this beauty, God could, in a certain sense, "rest." Fr. Sebastian Vazhakala, M.C., states this in a magnificent way:

> As God breathed on them [Adam and Eve] God's own breath, he also breathed on them the spirit of prayer [devotion to God's heart]. Prayer [devotion] then is very natural to human beings. It is not strange for humans to pray [have devotion to God]. It is just the opposite. Namely, it is very strange when human beings do not pray, do not acknowledge and accept God as their Creator.... St. Augustine calls it simply "Desiderium naturale", or better, the yearning of the human heart for God, for its Creator.... Psalm 42 expresses so vividly and so emphatically the normal experience of the human soul for its Creator: "Like a deer that yearns for running streams, so I long for you, my God. I thirst for you, the living God [Ps. 42:1–2]."[5]

Thus, we see in the seventh-day covenant, supported in Psalm 42, a natural and essential devotion to the love of God, to His Sacred Heart. God stressed that the heart would be a sign of covenantal love for both God and man even before the Incarnation. In Hebrew, this word is *hesed*,[6] which is a deeper, covenantal love. Here are some examples of *hesed* from the Old Testament with covenantal love pertaining to man (all emphases mine):

> You shall love the LORD your God *with all your heart*.... *Keep these words that I am commanding you today in your heart.* (Deut. 6:5–6)

[5] Fr. Sebastian Vazhakala, *The M.C. Tree* (Pittsburg, PA: Dorrance Publishing, 2020), 42.

[6] For more information and for classes on God's *hesed*, I highly recommend the Catholic Bible School, which offers a four-year curriculum showing this hesed within the overall story of salvation and covenantal history. See https://catholicbiblicalschoolva.org.

> *Why should you harden your hearts* as the Egyptians and Pharaoh hardened their hearts? (1 Sam. 6:6)

> *I will write it on their hearts;* and I will be their God, and they shall be my people. (Jer. 31:33)

Then there are verses about "the heart of God," His hesed found in the Old Testament (all emphases mine):

> The LORD saw that the wickedness of humankind was great in the earth, and that every inclination of the thoughts of their hearts was only evil continually. And the LORD was sorry that he had made humankind on the earth, and it grieved him to his heart. (Gen. 6:5–6)
>
> *We already noted that the first time Scripture speaks about God's heart, it speaks of man's wickedness in wounding God's heart.*

> But now your kingdom will not continue; *the LORD has sought out a man after his own heart*; and the LORD has appointed him to be ruler over his people, because you have not kept what the LORD commanded you." (1 Sam. 13:14)
>
> *God's prophet Samuel tells King Saul that God will seek a new king, a man after his own heart, to replace Saul.*

> *I will give you shepherds after my own heart*, who will feed you with knowledge and understanding. (Jer. 3:15)
>
> *God's heart is that of a provider (a Father) and a shepherd.*

> I will rejoice in doing good to them, and I will plant them in this land in faithfulness, *with all my heart and all my soul.* (Jer. 32:41)
>
> *God is all in with His heart!*

Most of the verses focusing on God's "heart" speak of His heart being broken by humanity or of His being worried about them.

We also note that in speaking of hesed love, the first time the word "love" is specifically mentioned in the Bible is in Genesis 22:2:

> He said, "Take your son, your only son Isaac, *whom you love*, and go to the land of Moriah, and offer him there as a burnt offering on one of the mountains that I shall show you." (emphasis mine)

And the first time you hear the inspired word "love," it involves sacrifice. Thus, sacrifice becomes part of the divine definition of hesed love.

The Old Testament tells us that hesed, covenantal love, was part of God's original plan. This love includes several characteristics:

1. Man's love is meant to mirror God's love.
2. God has a provider's heart imaged in His being a Father as well as a shepherd.
3. Having hesed love means being all in and not withholding anything.
4. Hesed love is sacrificial.

The Old Testament reveals that love should involve resting in one another, as seen in the beginning of creation through covenant and sacrifice. However, we also see man's being stubborn and God's being "wounded" by the sins of man. This brings about a tension between God and man: man is constantly trying to fill his heart with things other than God, while God is continually trying to stop man from hurting himself by making false covenants. So in the Old Testament, there is an emphasis on covenant, fidelity, and justice.

The psalms, which are hymns about various experiences in life that affect the heart, offer a way to resolve this tension between the heart of God and the heart of man. The psalms mention the word *heart* more than 130 times. Some psalms involve happiness when speaking about the heart, such as Psalm 4:7: "You have put gladness in my heart more than when their grain and wine abound." In this, we see that God wants to put gladness in our hearts by uniting with them. Psalm 9:1 says "I will give thanks to the LORD with my whole heart; I will tell of all your wonderful deeds." A grateful heart gives joy to the heart of God.

We also see psalms about inspired discernment. "When you are disturbed, do not sin; ponder it on your beds, and be silent" (Ps. 4:4). Again, "We ponder your steadfast love, O God, in the midst of your temple" (Ps. 48:9). Thus, the psalms encourage us to reflect upon life's deepest realities.

The psalms also speak about sin. Psalm 40:12 says, "For evils have encompassed me without number; my iniquities have overtaken me, until I cannot see; they are more than the hairs of my head, and my heart fails me." Sin cuts deep into the human heart. It encompasses us so that we miss God before our very eyes. We cause God great pain in hurting ourselves by choosing sin.

However, mankind does start to turn back toward God. Psalm 10:17 states, "O LORD, you will hear the desire of the meek; you will strengthen their heart, you will incline your ear." God will strengthen the hearts of the meek. Meekness is being able to control our anger and not letting our anger control us. We are not meant to be doormats, but we are not to be raging hulks either. We must develop the ability to direct our emotions toward charity—and God is charity itself (see 1 John 4:8). This is the reason Psalm 37:4 says, "Take delight in the LORD, and he will give you the desires of your heart." The Lord wants us to choose Him so He can give us the blessings He intends for our hearts. Look at Psalm 4:5: "Offer right sacrifices, and put your trust in the LORD."

So far, we have focused on either God or mankind. Now we will look at how God begins to prepare man's hearts for renewal. Sin seems unconquerable, but it can be conquered, and hesed love will one day be fulfilled. Listen to the words of the prophet Zechariah:

> Thus says the LORD of hosts: Even though it seems impossible to the remnant of this people in these days, should it also seem impossible to me, says the LORD of hosts? Thus says the LORD of hosts: I will save my people from the east country and from the west country; and I will bring them to live in Jerusalem. They shall be my people and I will be their God, in faithfulness and in righteousness. (8:6–8)

God Himself would reach down and save us from drowning in—as the song artist Adele would sing—"the depths of [our] despair." Humanity would have to trust that God would reach down and give them the desires of their hearts. And God does reach down; He becomes Incarnate in the Person of Jesus Christ. Jesus is the solution. In Him, the justice and mercy of God meet. Remember the words of Pope St. John Paul II, that Jesus Christ is "the human face [and heart] of God and the divine face [and heart] of man."

Jesus is the connection between the Old and New Testaments and the bridge to hesed covenantal love. Scripture tells us that justice and mercy meet: "Great is your mercy, O LORD; give me life according to your justice" (Ps. 119:156). We hear Jesus Himself admonishing the scribes and Pharisees, who can represent all fallen humanity, "Woe to you, scribes and Pharisees, hypocrites! For you tithe mint, dill, and cummin, and have neglected the weightier matters of the law: justice and mercy and faith. It is these you ought to have practiced without neglecting the others. You blind guides! You strain out a gnat but swallow a camel!" (Matt. 23:23–24). Mankind was blind to covenantal love and could not find it, no matter how hard they tried. This echoes the words of the prophet Jeremiah in the book of Lamentations:

My soul is bereft of peace;
I have forgotten what happiness is;
so I say, "Gone is my glory,
and all that I had hoped for from the LORD." (3:17–18)

But God does not leave man in despair. He sends His Son.

In the Son, particularly in His heart, we see justice and mercy come together. In the greatest sermon of all time, the Beatitudes, Jesus tells us that the hearts of mankind are meant for blessings. He says, "Blessed are the pure in heart, for they will see God" (Matt. 5:8). He tells us again, "For where your treasure is, there your heart will be also" (Luke 12:34). He knows that mankind is enslaved to sin, and so it seems that God's hesed love is burdensome like a yoke. Thus, Jesus reminds us of the importance of coming under God's loving yoke to find peace. He says, "Take my yoke upon you, and learn from me; for I am gentle and humble in heart, and you will find rest for your souls" (Matt. 11:29). Then He shows mankind that He can put them under the Father's hesed love because He is close to the Father: "No one has ever seen God. It is God the only Son, who is close to the Father's heart, who has made him known" (John 1:18). The Father is not heartless. He cares! This is the reason Jesus tells His disciples, "Do not let your hearts be troubled. Believe in God, believe also in me" (John 14:1). A few verses later, Jesus reiterates this point: "Do not let your hearts be troubled, and do not let them be afraid" (John 14:27).

Scripture shows that when man turns from sin, this consoles Jesus' heart. Consequently, when man consoles Jesus, Jesus pours out His mercy upon him. Just as a human heart gives and receives blood, so too, the heart of Jesus (the human heart of man and the divine heart of God) both *receives consolation* from man and simultaneously *gives him consolation, seen as mercy*! Scripture shows this dynamic unity of justice and mercy, the consolation of God and man:

> Steadfast love and faithfulness will meet; righteousness and peace will kiss each other. Faithfulness will spring up from the ground, and righteousness will look down from the sky. The LORD will give what is good, and our land will yield its increase. Righteousness will go before him, and will make a path for his steps. (Ps. 85:10–13)

> Great is your mercy, O LORD; give me life according to your justice. (Ps. 119:156)

> Just so, I tell you, there will be more joy in heaven over one sinner who repents than over ninety-nine righteous persons who need no repentance. (Luke 15:7)

We see through Scripture that devotion to the Sacred Heart of Jesus and Divine Mercy meet in God's hesed love incarnate, Jesus Christ. These devotions are woven together in Scripture and so make a beautiful tapestry of grace. These devotions also come together in history, as will be explored in the next chapter.

3

The Heart of God in History

History is part of the fabric of life. It helps us to remember who we are by recalling our roots and foundations, but it also draws us into the most important story of all time. History is His story: the story of Jesus Christ and His Mystical Body, the story of our salvation.

Now, when I say "story," I am not talking about fiction but about the most real and important event that ever happened: our salvation. Sadly, various teachings have gone against the ultimate goal of mankind: the unity of God and man in the heart of Jesus Christ through His Divine Mercy. These deceptive teachings deny the goodness of God's tangible love and mercy. Hence, St. John tells us to be aware:

> Many deceivers have gone out into the world, those who do not confess that Jesus Christ has come in the flesh; any such person is the deceiver and the antichrist! (2 John 1:7)

> This is the antichrist, the one who denies the Father and the Son. (1 John 2:22)

Presented under clever disguises, false doctrines that deny God's love and mercy sound convincing. St. Paul warned us of these false teachings in his Second Letter to Timothy :

> In the presence of God and of Christ Jesus, who is to judge the living and the dead, and in view of his appearing and

> his kingdom, I solemnly urge you: proclaim the message; be persistent whether the time is favorable or unfavorable; convince, rebuke, and encourage, with the utmost patience in teaching. *For the time is coming when people will not put up with sound doctrine, but having itching ears, they will accumulate for themselves teachers to suit their own desires, and will turn away from listening to the truth and wander away to myths.* As for you, always be sober, endure suffering, do the work of an evangelist, carry out your ministry fully. (4:1–5, emphasis mine)

The devotions to the Sacred Heart and Divine Mercy keep us on the path of truth. They also enable us to do the work of evangelists by keeping others from heresies, whose roots are in the antichrist, and to dwell in God's hesed love. These heresies, which deny that the Word became flesh and go against the Father and the Son, weaken people by preventing them from embracing the heart and mercy of God. Therefore, history, like a good doctor, diagnoses these heretical illnesses and prescribes the necessary medicines.

The heresies and attitudes that have denied Christ are found in the twofold anti-Incarnational effects of Original Sin: man's belief that he determines good and evil and his lack of trust in God. These effects led to the heresies of iconoclasm and Jansenism, which wound the Sacred Heart. The effects of Original Sin also bore the rotten fruit of modernism, a heresy that contradicts Divine Mercy. By looking at history's spiritual maladies, we can better digest the divine medicine given to us in the Sacred Heart and Divine Mercy devotions.

Salvation history begins with the Fall of humanity in the garden. Here the devil attacks humanity by instilling doubt. He tells them that man should determine good and evil. We read:

> Now the serpent was more crafty than any other wild animal that the LORD God had made. He said to the woman, "Did God say, 'You shall not eat from any tree in the garden'?" The woman said to the serpent, "We may eat of the fruit of the trees in the garden; but God said, 'You shall not eat of the fruit of the tree that is in the middle of the garden, *nor shall you touch it, or you shall die.*' " But the serpent said to the woman, "You will not die; *for God knows that when you eat of it your eyes will be opened, and you will be like God, knowing good and evil." So when the woman saw that the tree was good for food, and that it was a delight to the eyes, and that the tree was to be desired to make one wise, she took of its fruit and ate; and she also gave some to her husband, who was with her, and he ate.* Then the eyes of both were opened, and they knew that they were naked; and they sewed fig leaves together and made loincloths for themselves.
>
> *They heard the sound of the LORD God walking in the garden at the time of the evening breeze, and the man and his wife hid themselves from the presence of the LORD God among the trees of the garden.* But the LORD God called to the man, and said to him, "Where are you?" He said, "I heard the sound of you in the garden, *and I was afraid*, because I was naked; *and I hid myself.* (Gen. 3:1–10, emphasis mine)

Man's choices wounded his relationship with God. These wounds would be foundational to the attacks against the Sacred Heart of Jesus and Divine Mercy. First, we notice that Eve, in being tempted by Satan, exaggerates God's "justice" by adding words to God's command. We read in Genesis 2:16–17, "The LORD God commanded the man, 'You may freely eat of every tree of the garden; but of the tree of the knowledge of good and evil you shall not eat, for in the day that you eat of it you shall die.' " But note that in Eve's account to the devil, she adds to God's word by telling the devil, "We shall not eat of the tree or even touch it." And thus, Eve sees God as being harsh rather than being merciful. It also shows that Eve is trying to determine what is good and evil by adding to the definition of what God defined as evil, putting herself over God and thus changing the definition of love.

The second way the Fall builds a foundation for anti-Incarnational heresies is through man's desire to grasp for things beyond God's plan—i.e., lack of trust in God. After Eve converses with the devil, she looks at the fruit and once again sees an anti-Incarnational benefit. The food was always good, but now Eve adds to it that it is pleasurable and "desired to make one wise." Humanity goes from seeking what is good and loving, which is godly, to what is pleasurable—what is good for me alone. This outlook contradicts the very nature of God's love, which humanity was meant to image (see Gen. 1:26), and thus blurs God's sacred love in their hearts. Adam and Eve are not content with God's plan. In this, they proclaim that walking in God's love is not good enough. They wanted "to be wise" in ways other than God's ways—i.e., wise in the ways of the world. They put their trust in this new "worldly wisdom" instead of God's wisdom. Thus, they laid down another foundation against trusting in God.

In addition to humanity's attempts to determine what is good and evil and their grasping for things, they also severed their relationship with God through Original Sin. This is the final anti-Incarnational viewpoint. After Adam and Eve eat the forbidden fruit, they hide from God. This breaks God's heart because humanity no longer sees Him as a friend, as someone who loves them and looks out for them. They now see Him as an enemy, someone who is looking to punish or destroy them, someone who hates them. This false definition of God makes them decide that God, Goodness Himself, is evil. This is the ultimate and foundational sin that is rooted in fallen humanity. Reality shifts from living in love to living in fear. Thus, since they fear, Adam and Eve no longer trust God and do not run to Him for help (as both should have done in the first place); instead, they run from Him because they do not think He has any "heart" or mercy.

God's love should be the solid foundation for humanity, but Original Sin lays down a faulty and detrimental cornerstone. Original Sin states that humanity decides good and evil. In deciding good and evil, humanity could add words to God's commands, living not for the universal good, which is love, but for personal pleasure. Original Sin makes humanity hide from God instead of dialoguing with Him. And these diseases of Original Sin wound God's heart. Because of Original Sin, humanity no longer fully trusts God. Sadly, they distort God's word by imagining God as harsh; they do not trust God's wisdom but put their trust in *worldly wisdom* by desiring to know what is good and evil. This leads to living in fear instead of in love; not trusting in God's mercy but trying to hide from His "harsh justice." These would be the building blocks against Divine Mercy. These false beliefs would give mankind a "heart of stone" rather than a "heart of flesh" (see Ezek. 36:26).

We see these false notions come to fruition in Church history. Devotion to the Sacred Heart started in the early Middle Ages, but before that, the Church spent centuries clarifying, in various ecumenical councils, who and what Jesus Christ is. The ecumenical Council of Nicaea in AD 325 dogmatically refuted Arianism, which claimed that Jesus is merely God's highest creature. The council defined Jesus as truly God and truly man (with a human nature). The Council of Ephesus in AD 431 dogmatically defined that Mary is the Mother of God, that God came into history and took on flesh. This means that Jesus is both "true God and true man, consubstantial with the Father," as stated in the Nicene-Constantinopolitan Creed, which we pray at most Sunday Masses.

This Creed has practical applications. According to a theological concept called the "communication of idioms," what is said about Jesus' humanity (one of His natures) can also be said about the Person of Christ. This is because the human and divine natures are united in the second Person of the Trinity, who is Jesus Christ. This unity of human and divine natures in the hypostasis of Jesus Christ is called the Hypostatic Union. Thus, one can say "God was hungry" in Christ. "Mary is the Mother of God" because she gave birth to the Person of Jesus, not simply to His human nature. "God suffered" because Christ suffered on the Cross. "God wept and can be consoled" because of Christ's humanity. We now have the foundation for a devotion to the suffering Christ, who could be consoled by the hearts of mankind in the communication of idioms.

We should also point out that the communication of idioms does not change or alter the divine nature or the other Persons of the Trinity. For example, to say that "God suffered" or "God wept" does not mean that the divine nature as such "suffered" or "wept," or that the other Divine Persons (Father and Holy Spirit) "suffered" or "wept." Rather, it is the Person of the Word, Jesus Christ, who underwent suffering and thus can be consoled.

Thus, we look at the first heresy that opposed devotion to the Sacred Heart of Jesus—namely, iconoclasm. This heresy rose in the East during the 700s and beyond (eight and ninth centuries) and denied the essential element of Christ's humanity—His material nature. Iconoclasm said that God is transcendent and that it is wrong to limit Him to material things. Thus, statues and all material depictions of the divine were smashed. Devotion to the humanity of Christ, in particular His Sacred Heart, was suppressed and stunted. Remember, the antichrist is one who denies that Christ has come in the flesh (2 John 1:7). So this heresy promoted an antichrist perspective.

Then came St. Francis of Assisi, who lived in the 1200s. He saw God's beauty in creation, in the material world. He became a living reminder of Romans 1:19–20: "For what can be known about God is plain to them, because God has shown it to them. Ever since the creation of the world his eternal power and divine nature, invisible though they are, have been understood and seen through the things he has made." If material creation can tell us something about God, then God's material body would be able to reveal tremendous things about Him. This is the reason St. Francis of Assisi was so devoted to Christ's birth and His death. He created the first crèche and promoted the Stations of the Cross, which the Franciscans (his religious order) would oversee. St. Francis also received the stigmata of Christ—a sign that Jesus wanted to share His life with him, a deacon, a servant of mankind. In this act, Jesus is consoled by sharing His wounds with mankind. Thus, there is a historical precedent and an emphasis on consoling Christ.

St. John Eudes (1601–1680) continued St. Francis's desire to console Christ. He founded the Congregation of Jesus and Mary (the Eudists) at Caen in 1643. It consisted of diocesan priests not bound by vows but dedicated to improving the clergy by establishing effective seminaries and preaching missions. This foundation was opposed by the Jansenists (the group that would promote the major heresy against the Sacred Heart of Jesus). The Eudists sought to make the love of Jesus and Mary present in the world. It is interesting to note that during the process of St. John Eudes's canonization, Pope St. Pius X named him "the father, doctor, and apostle of liturgical devotion to the hearts of Jesus and Mary …

because he created the first Feast of the Sacred Heart in 1672, *just one year before St. Margaret Mary Alacoque had her first apparition of the Sacred Heart*" (emphasis mine).[7] From this first liturgical feast of the Sacred Heart of Jesus, celebrated within St. John's congregation, the Church would start to teach officially what was held dear from the altar of God. *Lex orandi, lex credendi*—the law of praying is the law of believing; in other words, what the Church does in her public prayers (liturgy) is what she believes (as articles of faith). This is a reason liturgy is important; it is a pedagogy of teaching. The primary reason for liturgy is the glory of God, and we give greater glory to God when we conform ourselves to what He has revealed and allow Him to work in and through us. This allows us to glorify God not simply with our humanity but with our humanity united to Jesus, who gives glory to God the Father through the Holy Spirit. Thus, the Church started to teach through her liturgy that the humanity and heart of Christ deserve respect and the adoration due to God.

This brings us to the anti-Christological heresy of Jansenism. Promoted by the heretical bishop Cornelius Jansen, this heresy was popular from 1640 to 1800. Todd Aglialoro of Catholic Answers describes this heresy:

> Jansenists hold that concupiscence (the tendency toward sin) always defeats the will in a fallen state. In those to whom God gives his grace, the will is equally powerless against this grace. The soul without grace will always be defeated by sin (and thus be damned), while the soul with grace will always be overwhelmed by it (and thus be

7 "St. John Eudes," The Eudists, https://www.eudistsusa.org/st-john-eudes.

> saved).... *Jansenists further insisted, contrary to orthodox Thomistic understanding, that God actively destines some to receive grace and actively destines others to be without it. One conclusion is that God will damn those who sin, even though they were never given grace to resist sin.* Conversely, those who receive grace cannot resist it and cannot avoid the workings of grace (sanctification)—a Fundamentalist would say they are "eternally secure." *Thus men are left "out of the loop" of their salvation, locked into a destiny which they cannot alter.* (emphasis mine)[8]

In other words, according to Jansenism, it does not matter what we do; the heart of Christ is cold and indifferent. Our sins define us, period. We see this in comparing the Catholic crucifix to a Jansenist cross. A Catholic crucifix has Jesus' arms outstretched in sacrifice and love for mankind. A Jansenist cross, however, has Jesus with one hand nailed to the Cross and the other pointing down, condemning a person for his sins. A person is labeled as a sinner or simply a slave. At its core, Jansenism attacks God's love for humanity. Many people adopted this false view of God's love because they thought that if someone is predestined for damnation or salvation, it does not matter what he does morally. This brought about a lot of despair and other grave sins that wounded Jesus' heart.

This false definition of God's love was so egregious to Jesus, who is truth (John 14:6), that He countered with devotion to His Sacred Heart. On October 4, 1673, the Lord appeared to a young novice of the Order of the Visitation named Sr. Margaret Mary Alacoque. He gave her as "her soul's guide" St. Francis of Assisi,

[8] Todd Aglialoro, "Jansenism," *Catholic Answers Magazine*, June 1, 1994, https://www.catholic.com/magazine/print-edition/jansenism.

the one who promoted the gospel of seeing God in His creation and who touched the heart of Christ so much that he received His wounds so their hearts could beat as one.[9] A few months later, on December 27, 1673, the Lord appeared again to St. Margaret Mary and revealed the devotion to His Sacred Heart. She wrote:

> "My divine heart," He told me, "is so passionately fond of the human race, and of you in particular, that it cannot keep back the pent-up flames of its burning charity any longer. They must burst out through you and reveal my heart to the world, so as to enrich mankind with my precious treasures."[10]

Jesus appeared to St. Margaret Mary a total of four times, entrusting her with the important mission of stopping the antichrist's lies. One of the chief lies is that God does not love man but cruelly creates him and labels him as according to his sins, faults, and failings.

Devotion to the Sacred Heart corrects these two major heresies of iconoclasm and Jansenism. It refutes the lie of iconoclasm by stating that God does speak through His creation—and, indeed, speaks a beautiful Word, His Word Jesus Christ, Love Incarnate. It shows that the body and the humanity of God are good; thus, all humanity is good—worthy of love, of redemption, and of respect. The Sacred Heart devotion also counters the horrors of Jansenism by showing that mankind is not just their sins. Pope St. John Paul II tells us that "we are not reduced to our faults and failings" but are the beloved of God.[11] God so loves humanity that He not only gives them a

[9] O'Donnell, *Heart of the Redeemer*, 128.

[10] Ibid., 131.

[11] Quoted in Daniel McCormick, "Your Life Is a Gift," *OneVoice*, October 28, 2021, https://onevoicebhm.org/your-life-gift.

participation and choice in their salvation (contrary to Jansenism) but also invites them to console Christ's Sacred Heart.

The deception of the antichrist did not stop at Jansenism, however. The good news is that neither did God's medicinal love. God would reveal another devotion, the Divine Mercy devotion.

With the World Wars, there was not only political turmoil but also spiritual turmoil. This involved the heresy of modernism, which became rampant then and continues today. Pope St. Pius X described modernism as "the synthesis of all heresies"[12] because modernism believes that the Church can "evolve"—a notion influenced by Darwinism, which also emerged at that time. People could therefore put their trust in progress to solve all the problems of humanity. People put their trust in war and political power; World War I was called "the war to end all wars." Then people put their trust in government and in political systems such as fascism and Marxism. Pope Pius XI warned strongly against this:

> In a word, the Communists claim to inaugurate a new era and a new civilization which is the result of blind evolutionary forces culminating in a humanity without God. Hence We wish to expose once more in a brief synthesis the principles of atheistic Communism as they are manifested chiefly in bolshevism. We wish also to indicate its method of action and to contrast with its false principles the clear doctrine of the Church, in order to inculcate anew and with greater insistence the means by which the Christian civilization, the true *civitas humana*, can be saved from the satanic scourge, and not merely saved, but better developed

[12] Pope St. Pius X, encyclical *Pascendi Dominici Gregis* (September 8, 1907), no. 39.

> for the well-being of human society. See to it, Venerable Brethren, that the Faithful do not allow themselves to be deceived! Communism is intrinsically wrong, and no one who would save Christian civilization may collaborate with it in any undertaking whatsoever. Those who permit themselves to be deceived into lending their aid towards the triumph of Communism in their own country, will be the first to fall victims of their error. And the greater the antiquity and grandeur of the Christian civilization in the regions where Communism successfully penetrates, so much more devastating will be the hatred displayed by the godless.[13]

The world fell victim to the synthesis of all the heresies by putting its trust in everything besides God; the effects of Original Sin thus resurfaced in a magnified way.

For every heresy, the Divine Physician has a remedy. Enter a young nun named Sr. Maria Faustina Kowalska of the Blessed Sacrament of the Congregation of the Sisters of Our Lady of Mercy in Poland in the 1930s. The Lord revealed to her His message of mercy from 1931 to 1938. Once again, God directly intervened to answer a horrific heresy. This time it was modernism. The antichrist sentiment said trust in progress, trust in war, trust in the power of the state. The Divine Mercy image, which is part of this devotion, shows rays of mercy flowing from Jesus' Sacred Heart and bears these striking words: "Jesus, I trust in You." The Divine Mercy devotion answers the modernist heresy in three ways. First, it shows that peace comes only from trusting in Christ.

[13] Pope Pius XI, encyclical *Divini Redemptoris* (March 19, 1937), nos. 11, 7, and 58.

St. Faustina had these revelations between the First and Second World Wars, when the world was looking for peace, but ironically in all the wrong places. Peace comes not through domination but only through submitting to Jesus, who is God's mercy and love incarnate. Second, the devotion shows that we progress in society only if we go forward in love, in God's mercy, not in hatred and revenge (which would eventually be the motivation for World War II). Then finally, we see that to be truly modern, we must go back to our roots: God's love, in which His mercy subsists.

History is full of ideas that are rooted in the antichrist—lies that deny the Incarnation and the love of the Father and the Son (and the Holy Spirit). Unfortunately, fallen man's notion that humanity could determine good and evil led to the rotten fruit of iconoclasm and Jansenism, and man's lack of trust in God developed the poisonous fruit of modernism. These were uprooted by the Sacred Heart and Divine Mercy devotions. Let us look at these devotions of the Sacred Heart of Jesus and Divine Mercy and how they may bear good fruit in our lives.

4

Devotion to the Sacred Heart of Jesus

The devotion to the Sacred Heart of Jesus is a powerful one that renews the hesed covenantal love between God and man. This devotion consists of five basic elements, which renew humanity by restoring our relationship with the God who loves us.

Our Lord gave these five aspects of the Sacred Heart devotion to St. Margaret Mary in four apparitions. They consist of the following:

- Thirty-Three Visits (given during an apparition on December 27, 1673)
- The image of the Sacred Heart (enthronement and badge) (July 2, 1674)
- Nine First Fridays (July 1674)
- Thursday night Holy Hour (July 1674)
- The feast of the Sacred Heart (June 1675)

Devotion to the Sacred Heart must have personal applications because God is not an egotist who needs divine consolation to feel good. God ask us to console His heart so we can rest in Him, which is what is best for us. God is thinking about us even when He is asking for consolation. This is true love! The five magnificent aspects of this devotion help repair our relationship with Christ's Sacred Heart and lead us to love God even more. Let us look at each one.

The Thirty-Three Visits

The first aspect of the Sacred Heart devotion is thirty-three visits to the Lord. Thirty-three times during a specified time frame (daily, if possible, but especially on Fridays[14]), we can visit the Lord through prayer or in other people—remember, Jesus said, "Just as you did it to one of the least of these who are members of my family, you did it to me" (Matt. 25:40).

St. Margaret Mary received this revelation on December 27, 1673. Here is the apparition's fuller context so that we can get to the heart of this aspect of devotion:

> "My divine heart," he [Jesus] told me, "is so passionately fond of the human race, and of you in particular, that it cannot keep back the pent-up flames of its burning charity any longer. *They must burst out through you and reveal my heart to the world, so as to enrich mankind with my precious treasures.*
>
> Next, he asked for my heart. I begged him to take it; he did, and placed it in his own divine heart. He let me see it there—a tiny atom being completely burned up in that fiery furnace. Then, lifting it out—now a little heart-shaped flame—he put it back where he had found it. "There, my well-beloved," I heard him saying, "that's a precious proof of my love for you, hiding in your side a little spark from its hottest flames. *That will be your heart from now on; it will burn you up—to your very last breath.... And how have you been describing yourself up to the present: my slave? Well, now I'm*

[14] Sisters of the Visitation of Paray-le-Monial, *Thoughts and Sayings of Saint Margaret Mary* (Rockford, IL: TAN Books, 1986), 100–101.

> *giving you a new name: the beloved disciple of my Sacred Heart."* (emphasis mine)[15]

In this revelation to St. Margaret Mary, we see that the more someone consoles the Sacred Heart, the more beneficial it is to that person. Notice that Jesus says first and foremost, "Give me your heart." He wants a relationship with us. Then He points out the littleness of St. Margaret Mary's and our hearts compared with His. Our hearts may be as tiny as atoms in the plan of God, but that can still be a blessing in God's plan to change the world. As another great mystic, St. Catherine of Siena, says, "Be who God meant you to be and you will set the world on fire." Then notice that Jesus gives St. Margaret Mary a new heart, a new perspective on life. Finally, the relationship with Jesus is renewed. He says to her: *You are not just "my slave" or my servant; you have a new name: the beloved!* By consoling the heart of Jesus, we remember our primary identity, which is someone loved by God!

These benefits can be ours through the thirty-three visits to the Lord. These visits are simple yet powerful: we make visits to Jesus in the tabernacle or simply pause and say hello to Jesus thirty-three times in a day, a week, a month, or whatever the designated amount of time. The more we spend time with Jesus, the greater the benefits we receive. Namely, we receive a relationship and a new heart, inspired by the fires of divine love, to replace the cold, bored, or despairing hearts that we carry due to life's circumstances. This devotion also reminds us to live out our identity of being loved by God. This is important because so many people today feel isolated, unloved, confused, and without purpose. St. Teresa of Calcutta calls these feelings "spiritual poverty." She says, "Being

[15] O'Donnell, *Heart of the Redeemer*, 129–131.

unwanted, unloved, uncared for, forgotten by everybody, I think that is a much greater hunger, a much greater poverty than the person who has nothing to eat."[16] Mother Teresa then continues with a practical application of these thirty-three visits involving visiting God in the poor. These visits console the heart of Christ while uplifting individuals:

> Without suffering, our work would just be social work, very good and helpful, but it would not be the work of Jesus Christ, not part of the Redemption. All the desolation of the poor people, not only their material poverty, but their spiritual destitution, must be redeemed. And we must share it, for only by being one with them can we redeem them by bringing God into their lives and bringing them to God.[17]

Spiritual destitution must be redeemed or offered to God. And bringing it to God consoles His heart because it allows our relationship to develop unconditionally.

So let us aim to visit the Lord thirty-three times either in the Blessed Sacrament, in the quiet of our hearts (so our hearts can meet His heart—*cor ad cor loquitur*), or in the poor, as Jesus tells us, "Just as you did it to one of the least of these who are members of my family, you did it to me" (Matt. 25:40).

The Image of the Sacred Heart

The next aspect of the devotion to the Sacred Heart is the Sacred Heart image. We can promote this image by wearing it, putting it

[16] "Quotes by Mother Teresa—Poverty," All Saints and Martyrs, https://saintscatholic.blogspot.com/2018/11/quotes-by-mother-teresa-poverty.html.

[17] "Mother Teresa." AZ Quotes, https://www.azquotes.com/quote/550653?ref=desolation.

in a place of honor, or dedicating our families through a ceremony called a home enthronement.

This aspect of the Sacred Heart devotion was revealed in Jesus' second apparition to St. Margaret Mary, on July 2, 1674. This apparition is described as follows:

> Christ expressed this pain and sorrow to St. Margaret Mary, coming to her, not in fury and rage but in sadness and agony: "Behold the Heart which has so loved men that it has spared nothing, even to exhausting and consuming Itself, in order to testify Its love; *and in return, I receive from the greater part only ingratitude, by their irreverence and sacrilege, and by the coldness and contempt they have for* Me *in this Sacrament of Love.*" (emphasis mine)[18]

Jesus is not angry but is sorrowful because of man's ingratitude. Thus, He speaks of more ways to inspire people to come back to Him by promulgating the image of His Sacred Heart for people to gaze upon. The apparition continues:

> My Divine Master revealed to me that *it was His ardent desire to be known, loved and honored by men, and His eager desire to draw them back from the road to perdition, along which Satan is driving them in countless numbers*, that induced Him to manifest His Heart to men with all the treasures of love, mercy, grace, sanctification and salvation that It contains.... This Heart of God must be honored under the form of His heart of flesh, whose image He wanted exposed, and also worn

[18] Alec Gany, "Behold, this Heart that Loves So Much Yet Is So Little Loved," Clarifying Catholicism, October 18, 2019, https://clarifyingcatholicism.org/mariology-and-saints/behold-this-heart-that-loves-so-much-yet-is-so-little-loved.

> on me and on my heart.... *He promised to pour out into the hearts of all those who honor the image of His Heart all the gifts it contains in fullness, and for all those who would wear this image on their persons He promised to imprint His love on their hearts and to destroy all unruly inclinations....* Everywhere this holy image was exposed to be honored, He would pour fourth His graces and blessings. This blessing was, as it were, a final effort of His love. He wanted to bestow upon men during these final centuries such loving redemption in order to snatch them from the control of Satan, whom He intended to destroy. (emphasis mine)[19]

The Lord attaches great promises of grace to those who gaze upon the image of His heart. He does this for three important reasons. First, in gazing upon His image, we will think about Him more and want to spend more time with Him. Second, in gazing upon the heart of Christ, we will forget all the things that we direct our attention to that leave us empty. Lastly, the Sacred Heart image motivates us to become better lovers and so to accomplish great things for God.

The Sacred Heart image is also a remedy against two sentiments that stunt our spiritual growth. Two anti-Incarnational sentiments that many people fall into are being "spiritual" (love without action) and being "pharisaical" (action without love). Jesus tells us, "I am the way, and the truth, and the life. No one comes to the Father except through me" (John 14:6). Being "spiritual" and being

[19] Jacqueline Burkepile, "Visions of the Sacred Heart of Jesus: 4 Mystical Messages to St. Margaret Mary Alacoque," EWTN Great Britain, June 11, 2021, https://ewtn.co.uk/chpop-visions-of-the-sacred-heart-of-jesus-4-mystical-messages-to-st-margaret-mary-alacoque.

"pharisaical" try to deny Jesus as the truth because they attack the very nature of God's Trinitarian love (they deny "the Father and the Son"—see 1 John 2:22). They also do not aim at consoling the heart of Jesus but focus only on themselves to the exclusion of Jesus, who is the way of grace.

Imagine floating in a kayak down living waters (see John 7:38) coming from the heart of Christ. You have two paddles to stir you down the river. These paddles are faith and charity (action). If you only use one paddle, you go in circles and do not move along the way. Both paddles are needed to go down the river of grace, but unfortunately, many continue to go in circles by embracing being "spiritual" or "pharisaical." This, in return, leads to frustration, and that frustration separates us from the love of God and prevents us from consoling Christ's heart.

Faith alone, without charity, is "being spiritual." This is having "love" in your heart for God but not putting it into action. The Sacred Heart of Jesus image counters this mentality. The flame of the Sacred Heart goes outward to show that love is meant to be given away, not kept for oneself. This is the image of the Incarnation.

In the word *Incarnation*, you see *in* and *carne*, which means "flesh" or "meat." Jesus came in the flesh! If someone takes flesh or meat and holds a fire to it for a long period of time, it hardens and burns. It is the same thing if we direct the flame of our desires to ourselves alone. If we think only about "me and God" to the exclusion of doing something for Him—or, worse, doing it just for "me"—then our hearts harden and we become prideful, selfish, and narcissistic.

We do not want to be "pharisaical" either. This is doing things without heart. This is the empty religion that Jesus condemned and warned about:

> Woe to you, scribes and Pharisees, hypocrites! For you are like whitewashed tombs, which on the outside look beautiful, but inside they are full of the bones of the dead and of all kinds of filth. (Matt. 23:27)

The Pharisees appear to act righteously and glorify God. The problem is they have no love in their hearts—even love of God. They reduce religion to social work; remember that Mother Teresa warned about mistaking acts of goodwill for charity. In an article I wrote for the *Arlington Catholic Herald*, I explain the difference:

> When we think of charity, many think of things like being nice, providing food for people and making donations of money. These are actions of goodwill but are not necessarily charity. Charity is a theological virtue, which means it necessarily must involve God. We do many nice things based on goodwill but have less and less charity because we exclude God. We must ask ourselves while doing our niceties, "Are we keeping God in the equation?" If not, are we making the world a more charitable place or creating a society full of good-willed people, but absent of God?[20]

The Sacred Heart of Jesus beckons us toward charity, not simply goodwill, because charity is what will exist in Heaven, the place of eternal joy. In this world, which is not our true home, goodwill or pleasure alone cannot remove the effects of Original Sin. This is the reason the Sacred Heart emphasizes saving us from this place known as "Adam and Eve's paradise," where we can be tempted

[20] Gerard-Marie Anthony, "Embracing Mary's Heart for Modernity," *Arlington Catholic Herald*, June 15, 2023, https://www.catholicherald.com/article/columns/embracing-marys-heart-for-modernity.

to determine ourselves as good outside of God (goodness without charity). The Sacred Heart image is a reminder to animate the world, our families, and our lives with charity.

If we have sentiments of faith without acts of charity, we are being "spiritual." If our actions are motivated by love of ourselves rather than love of God, we are being "pharisaical." Both stunt our growth and keep us from embracing God's plans for our lives. These wound the beloved heart of Jesus and beg for consolation.

The image of the Sacred Heart counters these false sentiments. If someone wears it as a badge of honor, it can remind him of his duty of charity toward society and even himself. An example of this is becoming a member of the Pioneer Total Abstinence Association of the Sacred Heart.[21] Members of the association wear a badge of the Sacred Heart on their shirts and say a daily prayer of reparation for the sins of intemperance in the use of alcohol. Sins caused by drunkenness are like the thorns that hurt Christ's Sacred Heart, but they can be overcome through love in these acts and prayers of reparation.

The main way to embrace the Sacred Heart image is by enthroning the image in one's home. A home enthronement makes Jesus the King of one's home (it is also recommended to make Mary the Queen of one's home). This simple ceremony of prayers and preparation makes Jesus the head of the household and this consecration of self and family is very powerful. The family then puts an image of the Sacred Heart in a prominent place in their home as a sign of their enthronement.[22] It is an act of the will and so is an act of love. To those who enthrone His image in their homes

[21] There is more information on this association later in the book.

[22] For more information on Sacred Heart Enthronement, please go to: https://welcomehisheart.com/home-enthronement.

Jesus promises an abundance of graces, such as peace in their families and the softening of the most hardened hearts.

The image of the Sacred Heart is thus an aspect of Sacred Heart devotion that counters the sentiments of being "spiritual" or "pharisaical" and is expressed through movements and activities that promote the image, such as the Pioneer Total Abstinence Association and home enthronements.

The Nine First Fridays

Another part of the Sacred Heart devotion is the Nine First Fridays, in which on the First Friday of nine consecutive months, a person attends Mass and receives Holy Communion in reparation for the outrages and sacrileges against the Sacred Heart of Jesus.

The Lord asked for this devotion along with the 11:00 p.m. Holy Hour in July 1674. St. Margaret Mary described this practice as follows:

> Jesus Christ, my sweet Master, presented Himself to me, all resplendent with glory, with His five wounds shining like so many suns. From all parts of His Sacred Humanity there issued flames but especially from His adorable breast, which was like a furnace.
>
> Opening it, He showed me His loving and lovable Heart as the living source of those flames. *Then he revealed to me all the unspeakable marvels of His pure love, and the excess of love He had conceived for men from whom He had received nothing but ingratitude and contempt. "This is more grievous to Me," [Jesus] said, "than all that I endured in my Passion. If they would only give Me some return of love, I should not reckon all that I have done for them, and I would do yet more if possible.* But they have only coldness and contempt for all My endeavors to

> do them good. You, at least, can give Me the happiness of making up for their ingratitude, as much as you can. First, you are to receive me in the Blessed Sacrament as often as obedience will allow, no matter what mortification or humiliation it may entail. *Moreover, you are to receive Holy Communion on the First Friday of each month.*"[23]

Jesus asks St. Margaret Mary to receive Communion on nine First Fridays to make up for the ingratitude of humanity. Jesus says that man's coldness is more grievous to Him than His Passion! The extreme coldness of humanity breaks the heart of Christ, but once again Jesus thinks of mankind in asking for consolation. He promises that these Nine First Fridays will bring Him consolation and will also allow for humanity to be blessed even more abundantly. He said, "If they would only give Me some return of love, I should not reckon all that I have done for them, and I would do yet more if possible." God wants to bless us, but we must be open to His blessing by remaining in His divine love. Love, however, goes both ways, and that is why consolations lead to blessings and presence leads to consolation.

This two-way street of communication is the foundation for the fittingness of the Nine First Fridays as a cure for the ailment of man's ingratitude.

The number nine is significant, as it suggests a novena of First Fridays. Now, I cannot claim to know the mind of God—in fact, St. Paul tells us this very same thing: "For who has known the mind of the Lord? Or who has been his counselor?" (Rom. 11:34)—but I can show the fittingness of nine Holy Communions on First Fridays. First, we must understand that there were no superlatives

[23] Burkepile, "Visions of the Sacred Heart."

in the Hebrew language. Someone would not say, "It is the best"; instead, he would repeat himself to show the higher degree. This is the reason Jesus says things such as, "Amen, amen, I say to you, before Abraham came to be, I AM" (John 8:58, NABRE). He emphasizes the importance of His statement when He repeats "Amen." In the same way, a novena repeats three sets of three to emphasize the importance of the best, highest good, who is God in the Most Blessed Trinity.

Nine also is the number for novenas. Fr. William Saunders tells us, "In the Middle Ages, particularly in Spain and France, novenas of prayers were offered nine days before Christmas, signifying the nine months our Lord spent in the womb of our blessed Mother. These special novenas helped the faithful prepare for the festive, yet solemn, celebration of the birth of our Lord."[24] We see that novenas were used to remind people of the nine months of Mary's pregnancy with Jesus. Pregnancy emphasizes a relationship, a union of people, a communion for nine months. Nine Holy Communions are supposed to reinvigorate the relationship between God and man and hopefully remind us of the intimate union between Mother and Child, Mary and Jesus, and humanity and God. The prophet Isaiah emphasizes this beautiful, intimate connection:

> And you shall nurse and be carried on her arm,
> and dandled on her knees.
> As a mother comforts her child,
> so I will comfort you. (Isa. 66:12–13)

[24] Fr. William Saunders, "What Is the Role of Novenas Today?," EWTN, https://www.ewtn.com/catholicism/library/what-is-the-role-of-novenas-today-1098. This article appeared in the August 25, 1994, issue of the *Arlington Catholic Herald*.

God is Father as He is the giver of life, but He wants an intimate communion with us, which is symbolized through the vocation of motherhood.

Nine is also the number of days of the original novena, from the Lord's Ascension to Pentecost. Before ascending into Heaven, Jesus told His disciples to wait in Jerusalem for the coming of the Holy Spirit, and they gathered there with Our Lady in prayer for nine days. On Pentecost, the Holy Spirit descended upon Mary and the apostles, enkindling in them the fire of divine love. The Holy Spirit warms the chill in man's hearts as the hymn "Come, Holy Ghost" tells us:

> In you, with graces sevenfold,
> we God's almighty hand behold
> *while you with tongues of fire proclaim*
> *to all the world his holy name.* (emphasis mine)[25]

The novena to the Holy Spirit is a sign of melting "the coldness of mankind" that the Lord mentioned to St. Margaret Mary; it inspires boldness as it leads people to proclaim "his holy name" once again.

Why did Our Lord choose Friday for this devotion? Friday is the day Our Lord showed how much He loved us by dying on the Cross. Thus, the day has taken on infinite importance. And why First Friday? Because it calls to mind our dignity: God always thinks of us or puts us first "as the apple of his eye" (see Deut. 32:10). It also reminds us of how we should console God in following the commandments He has given us. Jesus tells us, "If you love me, you will keep my commandments" (John 14:15). The first and

[25] Verse 3 of "Come, Holy Ghost," Hymnary.org, https://hymnary.org/text/come_holy_ghost_creator_blest.

greatest commandment that He has given us is this: "'Hear, O Israel: the Lord our God, the Lord is one; you shall love the Lord your God with all your heart, and with all your soul, and with all your mind, and with all your strength.' The second is this, 'You shall love your neighbor as yourself.' There is no other commandment greater than these" (Mark 12:29–31). God wants mankind to console Him by remembering the most important thing in life—relationship with Him. He wants us to love Him in the best way by obeying the Great Commandment!

This obedience can bring such consolation to Jesus' heart that He attaches a special blessing to it. He says, "I promise thee in the excess of the mercy of My Heart, that Its all-powerful Love will grant to all those who shall receive Communion on the First Friday of nine consecutive months the grace of final repentance; they shall not die under My displeasure, nor without receiving the Sacraments; My Heart shall be their assured refuge at that last hour."[26] In this novena of First Fridays, God promises the greatest consolation, which is to die in a state of grace.

Thus, the First Friday devotion is an essential part of devotion to the Sacred Heart. It consoles Jesus' heart by honoring the day He died for us (Friday) and remembering the goodness of God's covenant with us.

The Thursday 11:00 p.m. Holy Hour

The Thursday 11:00 p.m. Holy Hour is a prayerful hour spent with Jesus (preferably in an adoration chapel) to make reparation for Jesus' abandonment in the Garden of Gethsemane. This

[26] "12 Promises of the Sacred Heart," Sacred Heart Apostolate, https://sacredheartapostolate.com/wp-content/uploads/2018/07/Why-Enthrone-An-Image-of-the-Sacred-Heart-trifold.pdf.

aspect of the Sacred Heart devotion was also given in July 1674. We already heard of mankind's ingratitude in the first part of this July apparition. Here is what Jesus told St. Margaret Mary about the Holy Hour:

> You are to receive Holy Communion on the First Friday of each month, *and every night between Thursday and Friday I will make you partaker of that sorrow unto death which it was My will to suffer in the Garden of Olives.* This sorrow will reduce you, without your understanding how, to a kind of agony more bitter than death. *To join with Me in the humble prayer which I then offered to My heavenly Father in agony you are to arise between eleven and twelve o'clock, and remain with Me upon your knees for an hour*, with your face to the ground, to appease the anger of My Eternal Father, and to ask of Him pardon for sinners. *You will thus share with Me, and in a manner soothe the bitter grief I suffered when my disciples abandoned* Me and I was constrained to reproach them that they could not watch with Me even for an hour. During that hour you are to do what I will teach you. (emphasis mine)[27]

A few things stand out here. Notice that the Thursday 11:00 p.m. Holy Hour joins St. Margaret Mary and each person who participates in it with Christ during His agony in the Garden. It is based on unity, companionship, and presence, which bring about consolation.

How can one be present to Christ during His agony in the Garden? Jesus is God, so He is not bound by time; He is greater than it. Time is one of God's creations. Jesus is God and man, and as man, He entered time and became the center of it; time

[27] Burkepile, "Visions of the Sacred Heart."

is literally measured by His life, with years designated as BC (before Christ) or AD (Anno Domini—Latin for "in the year of the Lord"). Jesus is outside time but also within it as He holds all time together. St. Paul's Letter to the Colossians reiterates this point: "For in him all things in heaven and on earth were created, things visible and the invisible, whether thrones or dominions or rulers or powers—all things have been created through him and for him. He himself is before all things, *and in him all things hold together*" (1:16–17, emphasis mine). We can think of time like a circle with Jesus at the center. That means all points in the circle of time are equidistant from Christ and must go through Him in order to get to another point on the circle. This "circular time," called kairotic time, revolves around a purpose, as opposed to the past, present, and future of chronological time. Professor Tim Knight explains:

> The ancient Greeks had two words for time: chronos and kairos. Where chronos is quantitative, kairos is qualitative. Chronos is about minutes; kairos is about moments.... Chronos time moves on inexorably and methodically.... Kairos is a window of time that requires an intentional, purposeful response.[28]

Our Holy Hours in 2024 can be just as effective in consoling Christ in the Garden as St. Margaret Mary's Holy Hours in the 1670s were, or as the apostles' hour with Him in the Garden of Gethsemane in AD 33 could have been. Thus, our prayers said on Thursday nights between eleven o'clock and midnight can bring comfort and consolation to the Lord. These prayers may

[28] Tim Knight, "Chronos vs. Kairos," A Call to Excellence, February 27, 2023, https://www.acalltoexcellence.com/chronos-vs-kairos.

have even been brought to the Lord by the angel who comforted Him during His agony:

> Then he withdrew from them about a stone's throw, knelt down, and prayed, "Father, if you are willing, remove this cup from me; yet, not my will but yours be done." [*Then an angel from heaven appeared to him and gave him strength.* In his anguish he prayed more earnestly, and his sweat became like great drops of blood falling down on the ground.] (Luke 22:41–44, emphasis mine).

This act of consolation is amazing! The Lord wants so much to be united with us that He even allows time to be stretched for us to do it. Our prayers can be carried to Jesus during His time of loneliness if only we make the time to do so. Let us comfort Our Lord every Thursday for an hour, remembering the words of the great Bishop Fulton Sheen: "If you give God your time, He'll give you His eternity."[29]

The Feast of the Sacred Heart

God wanted the feast of the Sacred Heart to be celebrated universally in the highest degree to make reparation for the many sins of the world and to pour out an abundance of grace. Our Lord revealed this in His fourth and last apparition to St. Margaret Mary, in June 1675:

> And [opening] to me His Divine Heart: "Behold this Heart which has so loved men that It spared nothing, even going so far as to exhaust and consume Itself, to prove to them

[29] "Fulton J. Sheen Quotes," AZ Quotes, https://www.azquotes.com/author/13447-Fulton_J_Sheen.

> Its love. And in return, I receive from the greater part of men nothing but ingratitude, by the contempt, irreverence, sacrileges and coldness with which they treat Me in this Sacrament of Love. *But what is still more painful to Me is that even souls consecrated to Me are acting in this way. Therefore I ask of you that the first Friday after the octave of Corpus Christi be dedicated as a feast in honor of My Heart, and amends made to It in an Act of Reparation offered to It and by the reception of Holy Communion on that day, to atone for the outrages It has received during the time It has been exposed on the Altars.* I promise you that My Heart will open wide and pour forth lavishly the influence of Its Divine love on all who will render and procure for It this honor." (emphasis mine)[30]

In this aspect of the Sacred Heart devotion, Jesus wants to make His heart part of *His story* on the Church's calendar. He wants His Mystical Body to recognize His great love. St. Paul explains: "For no one ever hates his own body, but he nourishes and tenderly cares for it, just as Christ does for the church, because we are members of his body" (Eph. 5:29–30).

Jesus also wants the Church to repent and return to His Sacred Heart. Notice, He addresses various outrages that can happen during Eucharistic adoration: indifference to prayer, talking to others, desecrating the Blessed Sacrament, and sacrilegious Communions—receiving Holy Communion in a state of mortal sin. This could include priests' offering sacrilegious Masses or carelessly distributing Holy Communion, performing irreverent liturgies (Jesus speaks specifically of this in the apparition), and even desecrating the Blessed Sacrament or using their office to

[30] Burkepile, "Visions of the Sacred Heart."

allow things that go against the love of Christ. Furthermore, the sins of consecrated souls are "more painful" to Jesus because those souls are His close friends, and they should know better.

Thus, Jesus asked for a solemnity to be put on the Church calendar, reminding everyone of the centrality of His Eucharistic Presence. This solemnity would bring about the utmost consolation for His Heart knowing that the entire Body of Christ would make reparation for the sins committed against the Holy Eucharist. This is a great act of love on behalf of humanity because liturgy is the highest prayer that we can offer. Liturgy is being united not just in my prayer but in the prayer of the Church, which is the prayer of Jesus to the Father through the Holy Spirit. It becomes a prayer of reparation to the entire Trinity.

This leads us to the second aspect of this solemnity, which is its intimate connection with Divine Mercy. Jesus promises an abundance of graces for souls who participate in this part of the devotion—by going to Mass and receiving Holy Communion on the solemnity of the Sacred Heart. I also recommend enthroning an image of the Sacred Heart in your home and renewing your family (or individual) consecration to the Sacred Heart and even doing a parish-wide Eucharistic adoration event on this solemnity.

The five aspects of the Sacred Heart devotion mentioned in this chapter all bring about various fruits in different ways, but they also embody two messages. The first message is that God wants us to be in communion with Him. The second is that we must make reparation for all the things that keep us and the world disconnected from Him. As St. Margaret Mary tells us our Lord said in His June 1675 apparition, "the Lord wants to pour out the lavishness of the land." One of these abundant graces is the Divine Mercy devotion, which we will explore in our next chapter.

5

Devotion to the Divine Mercy

Jesus promises an abundance of grace to humanity through devotion to His Sacred Heart, but especially in observing the liturgical feast of the Sacred Heart. In liturgy (remember, this is work on behalf of the people because Jesus does this work on our behalf to the Father through the Holy Spirit), God invites mankind into His work of love because God is love. Hence, in doing the work of consoling Jesus with devotion to His Sacred Heart, mankind is consoled by the mercy of God through the Divine Mercy devotion.

As we saw earlier, the Divine Mercy devotion refutes the anti-Incarnational heresy of modernism, which builds upon Original Sin and multiplies the things it encourages humanity to trust in instead of God. The Divine Mercy devotion rebuilds trust in God's Fatherhood and consoles the children of God, the Mystical Body of Christ, in five dynamic ways. These five aspects of the devotion were given to St. Maria Faustina Kowalska of the Blessed Sacrament between February 22, 1931, and October 5, 1938—the day of her death. When Jesus called St. Faustina, He said, "**In the Old Covenant I sent prophets wielding thunderbolts to My people. Today I am sending you with My mercy to the people of the whole world. I do not want to punish aching mankind, but I desire to heal it, pressing it to My Merciful Heart.**"[31] Fr.

[31] Faustina Kowalska, *Divine Mercy in My Soul: The Diary of Saint Faustina* (Stockbridge, MA: Marian Press, 2005), no. 1588. All

Chris Alar uses the acronym "FINCH" to help us remember these Divine Mercy aspects:

Feast

Image

Novena

Chaplet

Hour of Divine Mercy

Before we discuss these five aspects of the Divine Mercy Devotion, we must look at the anti-Incarnational sentiment behind modernism.

There are many aspects of modernism: putting the state over the Church, putting reason over divine revelation, and, most dangerous, trying to replace God with something that seems better. Let us look briefly at some excerpts from Pope Pius IX's *Syllabus of Errors*, which declares eighty ideas that have always been condemned by the Church but are promoted as "good" under modernism. Pope Pius IX also cites the Church documents that condemn these errors:

1. There exists no Supreme, all-wise, all-provident Divine Being, distinct from the universe, and God is identical with the nature of things, and is, therefore, subject to changes. In effect, God is produced in man and in the world, and all things are God and have the very substance of God, and God is one and the same thing with the world, and, therefore, spirit with matter, necessity with liberty, good with evil, justice with injustice. (Allocution *Maxima quidem*, June 9, 1862)
3. Human reason, without any reference whatsoever to God, is the sole arbiter of truth and falsehood, and

subsequent references to this work will be cited as *Diary*, with the paragraph number (e.g., Diary 122).

of good and evil; it is law to itself, and suffices, by its natural force, to secure the welfare of men and of nations. (Allocution *Maxima quidem*, June 9, 1862)

5. Divine revelation is imperfect, and therefore subject to a continual and indefinite progress, corresponding with the advancement of human reason. (Allocution *Maxima quidem*, June 9, 1862)
6. The faith of Christ is in opposition to human reason and divine revelation not only is not useful, but is even hurtful to the perfection of man. (Allocution *Maxima quidem*, June 9, 1862)
8. As human reason is placed on a level with religion itself, so theological must be treated in the same manner as philosophical sciences. (Allocution *Singulari quadam*, December 9, 1854)
15. Every man is free to embrace and profess that religion which, guided by the light of reason, he shall consider true. (Allocution *Maxima quidem*, June 9, 1862; *Damnatio Multiplices inter*, June 10, 1851)
16. Man may, in the observance of any religion whatever, find the way of eternal salvation, and arrive at eternal salvation. (Encyclical *Qui pluribus*, November 9, 1846)
40. The teaching of the Catholic Church is hostile to the well-being and interests of society. (Encyclical *Qui pluribus*, November 9, 1846; Allocution *Quibus quantisque*, April 20, 1849)
44. The civil authority may interfere in matters relating to religion, morality and spiritual government: hence, it can pass judgment on the instructions issued for the guidance of consciences, conformably with their mission, by the pastors of the Church. Further, it has the

right to make enactments regarding the administration of the divine sacraments, and the dispositions necessary for receiving them. (Allocutions *In consistoriali*, November 1, 1850, and *Maxima quidem*, June 9, 1862)

48. Catholics may approve of the system of educating youth unconnected with Catholic faith and the power of the Church, and which regards the knowledge of merely natural things, and only, or at least primarily, the ends of earthly social life. (Epistle to the Archbishop of Freiburg *Cum non sine*, July 14, 1864)
66. The Sacrament of Marriage is only a something accessory to the contract and separate from it, and the sacrament itself consists in the nuptial benediction alone. (Apostolic Letter *Ad Apostolicae*, August 22, 1851)
80. The Roman Pontiff can, and ought to, reconcile himself, and come to terms with progress, liberalism and modern civilization. (Allocution *Jamdudum cernimus*, March 18, 1861)[32]

Though the Church has frequently condemned modernism, the errors of the heresy continue to spread today in various forms.

Modernism's false teachings, however, impede our desire for God, who is truth and love. This is the very definition of *acedia*, or spiritual sloth, sometimes called "the noonday devil."[33] Acedia is called the noonday devil because the sun is at its hottest at noon

[32] Pope Pius IX, *Quanto Cura: Syllabus of Errors* (December 8, 1864), Papal Encyclicals, https://www.papalencyclicals.net/pius09/p9syll.htm.

[33] I highly recommend Jean-Charles Nault, O.S.B., *The Noonday Devil: Acedia, the Unnamed Evil of Our Times* (San Francisco, CA: Ignatius Press, 2013).

and zaps your spiritual energy without your realizing it.[34] Here is how the *Catechism of the Catholic Church* (CCC) boldly defines acedia: "Acedia or spiritual sloth goes so far as to refuse the joy that comes from God and to be repelled by divine goodness" (2094).

Acedia refuses the joy that comes from God and makes God's goodness repel us. If we think that science answers everything, then the idea of needing more than science would repel us. If we think that we can educate our children in everything except the Faith and think we are doing what is best for our children, this could lead to resistance to family prayer time or seeing religious education or Sunday Mass attendance as a waste of time. Acedia could lead to the belief that the government knows best, and therefore I can ignore the Church's moral authority. If society sees the Church as a threat to be destroyed, society would rather embrace secularism than be formed by the Church. If marriage is just a contract and the blessing from the Church an accessory, it would lead people to wonder "What's wrong with getting married outside the Church or without a sacred minister?" It would appear that anyone can make a contract. Finally, if man can follow any religion he likes and obtain salvation, what is to stop him from following a self-religion and believing what he deems as good and fulfilling instead of following the beloved Catholic Faith for salvation? All of these are practical applications of modernism, the greatest of all heresies.

God sees acedia as egregious, just as He did Jansenism. He does not want humanity dwelling in misery by trying to invent their own truth and way to happiness. He does not want families falling apart or having no say in how they are to grow together. God does not want people to put all their trust in things that will fail to satisfy them in this life and in the next! Thus, God has a sure remedy

[34] Ibid., 20, 28.

for acedia and modernism: the Divine Mercy devotion, practiced in five ways. Again, remember the acronym FINCH:

Feast
Image
Novena
Chaplet
Hour of Divine Mercy

Let us look at each aspect of the devotion.

The Feast of Divine Mercy

Interestingly, Our Lord's revelations to St. Margaret Mary ended with a feast to console His Sacred Heart. Now Our Lord builds upon it and gives us another feast. This time He consoles the hearts of humanity with the grace of removing all temporal punishment due to sin. Mankind can obtain this great grace by attending Mass on the first Sunday after Easter (the Second Sunday of Easter) while doing the things necessary to obtain an indulgence: going to Confession (within about a week before or after the date of the indulgenced act), receiving Holy Communion in a state of grace, and saying some prayers for the pope. The normal window of Confession can even be expanded past its normal fourteen days. Robert Stackpole, S.T.D., explains:

> To receive those special graces—"the complete forgiveness of sins and punishment" ... in other words, a complete renewal of baptismal grace in our hearts—all we need to do is to receive Holy Communion in a state of grace on Divine Mercy Sunday, with trust in our Lord's great mercy. Whether your last confession was 10, 20, 30, or even more days before Divine Mercy Sunday, as long as you do not have the stain of unconfessed mortal sin on your soul, then

> you are spiritually alive in Christ and able to receive His special grace from Holy Communion on that great feast day![35]

To understand the immense blessing this Feast of Mercy is, we must look at the nature of sin. "All wrongdoing is sin," as St. John tells us in his epistle, but there are varying degrees of sin: mortal and venial (see 1 John 5:17). Mortal sin kills God's life in the soul; venial sin injures that life, making it easier for us to commit sins that will destroy our relationship with God (through mortal sin). All sins take us away from love of God, neighbor, or self. Thus, for every sin someone commits, whether mortal or venial, he must take a step forward to come back from the darkness into the light of God. For example, if someone takes three steps back, he must take at least four steps to make progress and be in the light (three steps forward would get him back to where he was, and he needs an extra step to make progress beyond that). This "taking steps to make progress" is called temporal punishment and it is attached to *every sin*. Now, imagine if you had to pay a dollar for every uncharitable word you said over the last year. How much money would you have to pay? Now multiply that for your entire lifetime! And this is just uncharitable words. We have not even mentioned paying for the sins of using God's name in vain, lying, or those things that go on while trying to exit the Church parking lot! The point is that we owe a lot. And the Lord reminds us of this, "Truly I tell you, you will never get out [of Purgatory] until you have paid the last penny" (Matt. 5:26). Yes, many of us will spend time in Purgatory since we will have so much temporal punishment to pay back the debt of our sins.

[35] Robert Stackpole, "On Going to Confession before Mercy Sunday," The Divine Mercy, March 28, 2007, https://www.thedivinemercy.org/articles/going-confession-mercy-sunday.

On the feast of Divine Mercy, however, our debt is paid in full. Jesus promises that if we celebrate His Feast of Mercy and fulfill the conditions mentioned above, we will not simply have some of our spiritual debt forgiven. *All* will be forgiven if we fulfill Jesus' words. This means that if we were to die immediately after fulfilling the requirements for this feast, we would have no temporal punishment to undergo in Purgatory. Our Lord confirms this to St. Faustina:

> **My daughter, tell the whole world about My Inconceivable mercy. I desire that the Feast of Mercy be a refuge and shelter for all souls, and especially for poor sinners. On that day the very depths of My tender mercy are open. I pour out a whole ocean of graces upon those souls who approach the fount of My mercy. The soul that will go to Confession and receive Holy Communion shall obtain complete forgiveness of sins and punishment. On that day all the divine floodgates through which grace flow are opened. Let no soul fear to draw near to Me, even though its sins be as scarlet. My mercy is so great that no mind, be it of man or of angel, will be able to fathom it throughout all eternity.... It is My desire that it be solemnly celebrated on the first Sunday after Easter. Mankind will not have peace until it turns to the Fount of My Mercy.** (*Diary* 699)

Yes, all sins will be forgiven if we come to the fountain of mercy. For those who believe their sins are unforgivable, let this feast be a proof of God's great mercy. God wants us to come to His mercy.

The Divine Mercy Image

The Divine Mercy image reminds us of God's covenantal love and simultaneously combats modernism. Our Lord appeared to

St. Faustina and described the image in a way that counters the modernist sentiment of putting trust in the wrong things:

> **Paint an image according to the pattern you see, with the signature: Jesus I trust in You. I desire that this image be venerated, first in your chapel, and [then] throughout the world.** (*Diary* 47)

There are four key elements in this image that Jesus requests. First, in the image, Jesus touches His Sacred Heart to show the connection between devotion to His Sacred Heart and Divine Mercy and to show that He wants us to touch His heart and thus His mercy.

Second, two rays, one red and one white, flow from Jesus' heart. The two rays represent the blood and water that flowed from His side on the Cross. The rays also represent the Sacraments of Baptism and Holy Communion. Baptism cleanses us of all sin, and Holy Communion cleanses us of venial sin. In the Holy Eucharist, we receive the life-giving Body, Blood, Soul, and Divinity of Jesus. Baptism and Holy Communion are both Sacraments of Initiation, which make us fuller members of the Church. Thus, these two rays show that the Church is born (through Baptism and the Eucharist) from the heart of Christ. Jesus further explains the meaning of the red and white rays flowing from His heart:

> **The two rays denote Blood and Water. The pale ray stands for the Water which makes souls righteous. The red ray stands for the Blood which is the life of souls.**
>
> **These two rays issued forth from the very depths of My tender mercy when My agonized heart was opened by a lance on the Cross.** (*Diary* 299)

The rays represent righteousness and life. Both are active nouns. You must step into the water to be cleansed and you must move (even cell growth is movement) to have signs of life. God wants us to have life, which is the reason He attests to this fact by giving His signature.

The signature, "Jesus, I trust in You," is the third aspect of the image. A signature is a formal way of putting your name to some type of agreement, contract, or covenant. Jesus' signature, "I trust in You," means that if we take Him at His word, He will help us in every aspect of our lives. Money, fame, and occupations (the things that modernism says we should trust in alone) come and go, but Jesus is always there whispering to us or standing before us in His image, saying, "I can and will help you. Trust me." He says this directly Himself:

> **I promise that the soul that will venerate this image will not perish. I also promise victory over its enemies already here on earth, especially at the hour of death. I myself will defend it as My own glory.** (*Diary* 48)

Venerating the image and following the Lord's advice above involves an act of faith. For this act of faith, Jesus guarantees, by His signature fidelity, salvation and even victory over our enemies in this life. The signature represents acts of faith, but the blood and water show that this faith must be put into action.

This brings about the fourth aspect of the Divine Mercy image. Jesus is shown stepping forward, meaning that God initiates healing and consolation. We, in turn, must walk toward Him to be consoled, to really live out that trust.

Let us return to St. Faustina of the Blessed Sacrament, the Apostle of Divine Mercy, who, through her extraordinary graces of bilocation and her ability to read souls, shows us how to receive God's mercy.

St. Faustina experienced the grace of bilocation, which means that she could be in two places at once. We marvel at this gift, but actually, bilocation is simply being where God wants us to be. All of us should "bilocate" as we pray in the Our Father, "Thy Kingdom come; thy will be done on earth as it is in Heaven." Our body and actions are on this earth, but our mind should always be in a second place—in Heaven. In an analogous sense, all of us should live out the charism of bilocation by living out the Our Father.

St. Faustina could also read souls. We can be amazed at this as well, but God allows everyone to read at least one soul: our own—although we are often too busy to do so. How can we be healed if we do not take the time to read our souls and carry within them the Lord's signature, which leads to joy? This text, which is God's signature, brings us to the heart of the image: Jesus, I trust in You! This is what we must constantly have on our minds and hearts to guide our actions. This is what puts our faith into action and allows us to be consoled during the hardships of life. This is what counters acedia and makes us fervent in doing the will of God. So let us meditate often on the Divine Mercy image.

The Divine Mercy Novena

The Divine Mercy Novena generally starts on Good Friday and ends on the eve of Divine Mercy Sunday. It is nine days of prayer connecting the Cross of Christ to His mercy. On each day, a Chaplet of Divine Mercy (covered below) is said for a particular group of people. In this novena, the whole world and all the Church can be immersed in God's mercy and love.

The Divine Mercy Novena is also a reminder that we must be rooted in prayer. Without prayer, a person can, at best, be lukewarm because he is not plugged into the source of grace and virtue. Those who do not have friendship with the source of life, God Himself, can never be fully alive. God's dream for humanity is that they might share in His divine life, which is to experience true happiness. He wants us to be truly fulfilled, which is the reason lukewarm souls hurt His heart. Jesus told St. Faustina:

> **My soul suffered the most dreadful loathing in the Garden of Olives because of lukewarm souls.** (*Diary* 1228)

We can say this novena anytime during the year, but especially between Good Friday and Divine Mercy Sunday. St. Faustina writes, "The Lord told me to say this chaplet for nine days before the Feast of Mercy. It is to begin on Good Friday. **'By this novena, I will grant every possible grace to souls'** " (*Diary* 796).

During this novena, we pray for the following members of Christ's Mystical Body that they might encounter Divine Mercy:

- All mankind, especially sinners
- Souls of priests and religious
- Devout and faithful souls
- Those who do not believe in God and do not know Him yet
- Those who have separated themselves from the Church
- Meek and humble souls of children
- The souls who venerate God's mercy (notice this is on the covenantal day 7)
- The souls in Purgatory
- Those who have become lukewarm

God wants all of creation to embrace and be consoled with His mercy. Thus, the novena speaks of laity and clergy, the Church Militant (us here on earth) and the poor, forgotten souls in Purgatory, those who are in the Church and even those who have separated themselves from the Church, those who bring comfort to Christ as well as those who cause Him much pain, such as the lukewarm. Jesus wants all people to trust in Him and not label themselves as "hopeless causes" or people who despair rather than praise God's goodness:

> Jesus is commanding me to make a novena before the Feast of Mercy, and today I am to begin it for the conversion of the whole world and for the recognition of The Divine Mercy. . . . **"So that every soul will praise My goodness. I desire trust from My creatures. Encourage souls to place great trust in My fathomless mercy. Let the weak, sinful soul have no fear to approach Me, for even if it had more sins than there are grains of sand in the world, all would be drowned in the unmeasurable depths of My mercy."** (*Diary* 1059)

The Divine Mercy Novena reminds the world that "we are not reduced to our faults and failings" but are the beloved of God. We must help others dive into the ocean of God's mercy.

The Chaplet of Divine Mercy

The Chaplet of Divine Mercy is the most familiar aspect of the Divine Mercy devotion (see appendix 2 for instructions on how to pray the chaplet). While praying this devotion, we can meditate on Christ's five wounds and the value of suffering.

In Fr. Alar's book *Understanding Divine Mercy* is a great section called "The Key to Happiness Is Our Misery." This might sound strange at first, but when we pray the Chaplet of Divine Mercy, our misery rises to the surface to encounter God's mercy. In it, we offer the Father "His dearly beloved Son in atonement for our sins and those of the whole world." We invite the Trinity into all of our tasks as we repeat this prayer. God gives each of us different duties, and we must do His will in the present moment. What is God's will? It is our sanctification (see 1 Thess. 4:3). The Father also desires the consolation of His Son.

The Chaplet of Divine Mercy is one of the greatest ways to console the Son. As the beads slip through our fingers, we are given a tangible way to connect our misery to the Cross of Christ. This comforts His Sacred Heart and draws mercy down upon souls. Each bead is like an expression of gratitude or like embracing Christ during His agony in the Garden. When we are stuck in traffic … "For the sake of His sorrowful Passion, have mercy on us and on the whole world"; that's one ounce of comfort for the Lord during His agony. When our boss comes into our office and yells at us for no reason … "For the sake of His sorrowful Passion …" When breakfast falls on the floor or a food fight breaks out among the kids … "For the sake of His sorrowful Passion …" The consolation of Christ brings about the Father's mercy through the Holy Spirit: "Have mercy on us and on the whole world." Imagine how much consolation we could bring to Jesus' heart if we were to run those Divine Mercy Chaplet beads through our fingers during the day whenever we are inconvenienced or annoyed or interrupted.

The chaplet helps us realize that God's will may unfold differently from how we imagined it. This is the reason we ask for Jesus' help: "For the sake of His sorrowful Passion, have mercy on us and on the whole world." God's plan is always best, but we often try to run from it because we think our desires will be better than God's will for our lives. When we try to disobey or flee from God's will, it can cause misery because when we flee from God's will, we flee from God (God and His will cannot be separated). Thus, He appears distant or even absent. This appearance can come from our own choice (which often happens) or as a purgation that happens to us. *No matter the cause: We must be willing to give God our misery, so we can find His mercy.* St. Faustina writes beautifully:

> Jesus replied, **"My daughter, you have not offered Me that which is really yours."** I probed deeply into myself and found that I love God with all the faculties of my soul

> and, unable to see what it was that I had not yet given to the Lord, I asked, "Jesus, tell me what it is, and I will give it to You at once with a generous heart." Jesus said to me with kindness, **"Daughter, give Me your misery, because it is your exclusive property."** At that moment, a ray of light illumined my soul, and I saw the whole abyss of my misery. In that same moment I nestled close to the Most Sacred Heart of Jesus with so much trust that even if I had the sins of all the damned weighing on my conscience, I would not have doubted God's mercy but, with a heart crushed to dust, I would have thrown myself into the abyss of Your mercy. (*Diary* 1318)

When we can acknowledge our misery and entrust it to God's mercy, we make a true offering of ourselves to the Father. Many of us hold on to our misery, anger, and failures like nails to a cross. God says, "Let them go!" Give them to God's mercy. Christ did not stay nailed to the Cross forever. No, He rose again! We must place our misery in Christ's heart, leading us to trust in Him more fully, so that we can rise with Him.

St. Faustina shares a nugget of wisdom concerning what to ask for and what not ask for as it pertains to her own misery:

> O Living Host, support me in this exile, that I may be empowered to walk faithfully in the footsteps of the Savior. I do not ask, Lord, that You take me down from the cross, but I implore You to give me the strength to remain steadfast upon it. I want to be stretched out upon the cross as You were, Jesus. (*Diary* 1484)

May we use the chaplet to walk faithfully in our relationship with God.

The Hour of Divine Mercy

The Hour of Divine Mercy is from 3:00 to 4:00 p.m. As Jesus, when He died at 3:00 p.m. on Good Friday, entrusted everything to the Father, so in the Hour of Divine Mercy, a person entrusts everything to the Sacred Heart of Jesus. One can pray a Chaplet of Divine Mercy, a Rosary, a Holy Hour, and even make the Stations of the Cross, as Our Lord advised St. Faustina:

> **Try your best to make the Stations of the Cross in this hour, provided that your duties permit it; and if you are not able to make the Stations of the Cross, then at least step into the chapel for a moment and adore, in the Most Blessed Sacrament, My Heart, which is full of mercy: and should you be unable to step into the chapel, immerse yourself in prayer there where you happen to be, if only for a very brief instant.** (*Diary* 1572)

At 3:00 p.m., Jesus breathed His last and entrusted everything to the Father. So, too, in this hour, we unite ourselves to the Father through the Son and remember Jesus' ultimate sacrifice. This is the hour of trust (against modernism and acedia) and during this hour, the Lord wishes to bless us for our fidelity:

> **At three o'clock, implore My mercy, especially for sinners; and, if only for a brief moment, immerse yourself in My Passion, particularly in My abandonment at the moment of agony. This is the hour of great mercy.... In this hour I will refuse nothing to the soul that makes a request of Me in virtue of My Passion.** (*Diary* 1320)

The Lord asks us simply to give Him a little time. The Hour of Mercy is a crucial reminder that we must not be too busy. BUSY is an acronym for "buried under Satan's yolk," and this is one of the bitter fruits of modernism. We become so busy with a million and one things to do that we forget the one thing that really matters: our relationship with God. We become too busy to be blessed. The Lord offers graces of conversion, healings of mind, body, and soul, but we do not ask for them. Why? Because we are too busy! The Hour of Mercy is the time to ask for the greatest graces so we can be consoled by Jesus Christ.

Make no mistake, the Divine Mercy devotion is the antidote to the anti-Incarnational heresy of modernism and the poisonous sentiment of acedia. The feast of Divine Mercy consoles us by giving us an indulgence that pays for all temporal punishment due to sin. The Divine Mercy image reminds us that God has not abandoned us but is walking toward us and guarantees this with His signature, "Jesus, I trust in You." The Divine Mercy Novena reminds us that Jesus wants to console the world, no matter what our state in life and no matter how far from Him we may be. The Chaplet of Divine Mercy reminds us that every moment can be a source of consolation to Jesus' heart while He seeks to console our heart with His mercy. And the Hour of Mercy reminds us that we must not be too busy for God's consolations.

Let us now look at how the devotions to the Sacred Heart and Divine Mercy unite in one powerful message.

6

Bringing Devotions Together to Make Us New

The Sacred Heart and Divine Mercy devotions are separated only by time, just over 250 years. However, these two devotions reunite in our times to offer hope for humanity. These two most powerful devotions can rewrite history for future generations. Thus, we will look at the messages of both devotions and how they come together in an invigorating way.

The first thing of note is a string of numbers. We started off with five notions about God from Genesis concerning the biblical basis of the Sacred Heart. These five properties allow us to note the relations between the Persons of the Trinity; they are innascibility, paternity, filiation, spiration, and procession. Thus, the number five connects us to the three Divine Persons of the Blessed Trinity, whom we are meant to mirror.

Next, there are Jesus' five wounds: one in each hand, one in each foot, and one in His pierced side. These wounds reveal a profound truth: God takes on all our suffering so that we no longer need to live in fear or feel abandoned. Christ's hands were nailed to show us that we are called to imitate His example of service, as He came "not to be served but to serve and to give his life a ransom for many" (Matt. 20:28). His feet were nailed to show us the need to be still and bring people to God. His side was pierced with a lance so that we could embrace the life-changing blood that flowed from His side. Each of the five wounds has an important message for humanity.

Third, both the Sacred Heart and Divine Mercy devotions have five manifestations. These five particular aspects reveal that consoling Jesus' Sacred Heart leads to the manifestation of God's mercy. And these manifestations are similar: both devotions have a feast, an image, and an hour.

Fourth, there are five groups of works to console Christ's Heart (Christ the Head and Christ in His Mystical Body) and to immerse humanity in His life. These five works, which God uses to empower us, are the following: conversion, conservation, consolation of Jesus' Sacred Heart, consolation of Jesus' Mystical Body, and invitations to grace. I will address these later in the book. For now, we should see a common denominator, which is the number five.

The number five is important because it is the number for grace in Scripture and theology:

> The number 5 symbolizes God's grace, goodness and favor toward humans. The word "five" is recorded 345 times in Scripture. Since five represents grace, when it's multiplied by itself, it produces 25 which is "grace upon grace" (John 1:16).... There are five books of God's Law (Genesis, Exodus, Leviticus, Numbers and Deuteronomy) commonly referred to as the Pentateuch ("Penta" means five).... Holy anointing oil is mentioned in Exodus 30:23–25. Its ingredients, which were given directly by God, were used to consecrate the furniture of the tabernacle. It was comprised of 5 parts, as it was a revelation of pure grace.[36]

[36] "Meaning of Numbers in the Bible: The Number 5," Bible Study, https://www.biblestudy.org/bibleref/meaning-of-numbers-in-bible/5.html.

These fives represent Jesus, the "grace upon grace" whom we have received from the Father (see John 1:16). It is Jesus' Sacred Heart and Divine Mercy that console God and the Mystical Body.

This chart allows us to see the differences in the Sacred Heart and Divine Mercy devotions and their lasting effect on humanity.

	Sacred Heart	**Divine Mercy**
How the devotion consoles	We go to console Jesus	Jesus comes to console us
Basis	Based on the ingratitude of men	Based on the mercy of God
How the devotion reflects God's love	The love of God is made manifest, and reparation for sin is asked in justice	The love of God is poured out in mercy because of grace
Heresies that the devotion combats	Against Jansenism and iconoclasm	Against modernism
Poisonous attitudes that the devotion overcomes	Being merely "spiritual" or "pharisaical"	Acedia
The false view from Original Sin that the devotion repels	Man's attempt to determine what is good and evil	Lack of trust in God's Fatherhood

Although these devotions are different, they beautifully complement each other. Devotion to the Sacred Heart is a consolation of Jesus' heart for the ingratitude of men. The Divine Mercy devotion is a consolation of humanity based on the graciousness of God. The purposes of both consolations are based on hesed love, in which participants in the covenant want to comfort and stay in each other's presence. This theme of presence runs throughout Scripture. Here are some examples:

> And the Word became flesh and lived among us, and we have seen his glory, the glory as of a father's only son, full of grace and truth. (John 1:14)

> "Look, the virgin shall conceive and bear a son, and they shall name him Emmanuel," which means, "God is with us." (Matt. 1:23)

> And I heard a loud voice from the throne saying, "See, the home of God is among mortals. He will dwell with them; they will be his peoples, and God himself will be with them; he will wipe every tear from their eyes. Death will be no more; mourning and crying and pain will be no more, for the first things have passed away." (Rev. 21:3–4)

God's heart and mercy come together in a mutual consolation of presence!

Presence is equal to love because, as someone famously said, "How do you spell love? The answer: T-I-M-E!" Time is the necessary ingredient for love, and when we invite the love of God into our time, we get His eternity. Thus, we look at God's love in these two devotions. In the Sacred Heart devotion, the love of God is made manifest, and reparation for sin is asked in justice. The focus is on God's justice. Many see God's justice, however, as involving a master-servant relationship with us. The Sacred Heart devotion tells us of a different and more elevated type of justice—one of a Father and child. A child owes his parents not only respect but, more importantly, love. This is explained in the statement "There are no grandchildren in Heaven." At first, this sounds scary, but it is the perfect explanation of this kind of justice caught up in love. The most important relationship that will get us into Heaven is our covenantal relationship with God. Every other relationship is subordinate to this. It is not our relationship with our parents, grandparents, teachers, pastors, or anyone else that will get us into Heaven but only our own personal, covenantal relationship with God. Each of us must live as a child of God. This is the justice that God asks for, which consoles Jesus' Sacred Heart.

In the Divine Mercy devotion, we look at a different aspect of God's love: His mercy. The love of God is poured out in mercy because of grace—not because of something we earn (ironically, this would be a Pelagian and Jansenist point of view) but because we are His children, and He wants us to be one with Him. As St. Paul tells us, "Indeed, rarely will anyone die for a righteous person—though perhaps for a good person someone might actually dare to die. But God proves his love for us in that while we still were sinners Christ died for us" (Rom. 5:7–8). The Sacred Heart devotion focuses on justice and relationship. The Divine Mercy devotion focuses on mercy and grace. Therefore, justice embraces mercy, and relationship is taken up into grace.

This brings us to the heresies and poisonous sentiments that the Sacred Heart and Divine Mercy devotions combat. The Sacred Heart devotion combats Jansenism, which identifies us with only sin, closing our access to God's love. The Sacred Heart devotion proclaims that God's heart has been opened literally for all to touch and console Him. This is the antidote to a "spiritual" relationship in which we think we love God but never live out that love. The Sacred Heart devotion is also the antidote to a "pharisaical" mindset, in which we perform good works without God; this means there is no charity in our works since charity is a theological virtue. A world without God, without charity, would not be a good world! It would, in fact, be an evil world because evil is the absence of good, according to St. Augustine. The greatest evil would be a place without the greatest good, who is God. Thus, devotion to the Sacred Heart combats efforts to make the world good without God—which results only in perpetuating the greatest evil on earth.

The Divine Mercy devotion combats modernism, which makes mankind trust in things other than God. Modernism also attacks people's ability to desire God in their lives, to begin anew with God. This brings about acedia, which makes man slow in doing things that will strengthen his relationship with God. Modernism's ultimate goal is to be so "modern" or "progressive" that man will eventually not only forget God but will replace Him with himself or some "righteous cause."

The Sacred Heart and Divine Mercy devotions proclaim boldly that we should live with God, for only in our receiving His love can "all things … be restored in Christ" (see Eph. 1:10). People devoted to the Sacred Heart and Divine Mercy testify that a "godless world" is a world that God does not will and does not want His children to live in. In combating heresies and sentiments that bring about an atheistic, godless world that degrades mankind, the Sacred Heart and Divine Mercy devotions make mankind fully alive—and this consoles God.

These two powerful devotions get to the root of moral problems in our times by exposing the false views associated with Original Sin. Man realizes that it is not his heart but the Sacred Heart of Jesus that determines good and evil. And since we are not just our faults and failings but are children of God, He can pour out His mercy upon us. These devotions also combat the lack of trust in God because we see that God not only provides for us but provides "grace upon grace." He does not make us and then let us fend for ourselves, as deism believes. God is a Father. He is merciful. And He gives us His heart. We just have to trust Him.

Reflecting on how God has shown His continuous fidelity in Scripture, in history, and in our lives will strengthen our trust. But sometimes we need to trust even when it doesn't seem easy. Charles Blondin shows us that trusting in God and consoling His Sacred Heart are like walking a tightrope.

> Many years ago, the story goes, a man named Blondin strung a tightrope across Niagara Falls and proceeded to traverse the raging waters. A crowd gathered as he successfully made his way back to his starting place. "Who here believes I can cross over Niagara Falls again, but this time pushing a wheelbarrow?" The exhilarated crowd began shouting, "We believe, we believe!" And sure enough, Blondin steered the wheelbarrow successfully across the Falls and back, to the riotous applause of the onlookers! "Who here believes I can cross over Niagara Falls a third time, but this time with a man in the wheelbarrow?" The crowd could barely control their enthusiasm, so spectacular were the achievements of this death-defying aerialist. "We believe! We believe!" they roared, all the louder. Blondin replied, "Okay, then who will be my first volunteer in the wheelbarrow?" Silence.[37]

[37] Dan Flynn, "Wheelbarrow: A Parable of Faith," God Can, God Cares, May 26, 2020, https://godcangodcares.com/wheelbarrow-a-parable-of-faith.

The Sacred Heart of Jesus and Divine Mercy devotions encourage us to get into the wheelbarrow of God's love! God wants to carry us across the great mountains and valleys of life, but we must let Him. We must believe that He has given His heart to us without reservation, manipulation, and condemnation, and this will lead us to trust in Him with confidence, integrity, and faith. Then the world will be transformed from Hell on earth (the absence of God) to Heaven beginning on earth because "where there is God, there is love."[38] Where there is love, there are the seeds of Heaven!

[38] This is the motto of a great apostolate: the Mother of Light Center, which helps the poor. See https://www.motheroflightcenter.com.

7

Consolation in Prayer and Activation through Mercy

God gives us the gifts of faith, hope, and love in Baptism. To be rooted in faith and hope and to live out love, we need prayer. Prayer brings us consolation and, by allowing God into our lives, brings Him consolation. Moreover, prayer makes us new, as the prophet Haggai illustrates in the following parable:

> Thus says the LORD of hosts: Ask the priests for a ruling: If one carries consecrated meat in the fold of one's garment, and with the fold touches bread, or stew, or wine, or oil, or any kind of food, does it become holy? The priests answered, "No." Then Haggai said, "If one who is unclean by contact with a dead body touches any of these, does it become unclean?" The priests answered, "Yes, it becomes unclean." Haggai then said, *So is it with this people, and with this nation before me, says the LORD; and so with every work of their hands; and what they offer there is unclean.* (2:11–14, emphasis mine)

I will use a modern analogy to explain Haggai's oracle. If Haggai has a clean pen and puts it on a dusty podium, does the pen make the podium clean? No. Now, if he puts a muddy pen on a clean podium, does the pen make the podium dirty? Yes. This is the same with the things of God. Empty worship is not pleasing to God. The dirty hearts of Judah and their priests in Haggai's time will not make their sacrifices "clean" or pleasing to God. Nor will the dirty or empty hearts of modernity make us clean. This was Cain's problem; he tried to offer a saving covenantal sacrifice despite his impure heart. It would be like our saying, "We're Catholic" without living the Faith. This was what God was trying to awaken in the mind of humanity through devotion to the Sacred Heart.

But, says the prophet Haggai, look at what mankind can do and at what God can do:

> But now, consider what will come to pass from this day on. Before a stone was placed upon a stone in the LORD's temple, how did you fare? When one came to a heap of twenty measures, there were but ten; when one came to the wine vat to draw fifty measures, there were but twenty. I struck you and all the products of your toil with blight and mildew and hail; yet you did not return to me, says the LORD. *Consider from this day on, from the twenty-fourth day of the ninth month. Since the day that the foundation of the LORD's temple was laid, consider*: Is there any seed left in the barn? Do the vine, the fig tree, the pomegranate, and the olive tree still yield nothing? *From this day on I will bless you.* (2:15–19, emphasis mine)

God says that, naturally, our stained sacrifices will continue to stain our people. We need to be fully united with God because He makes things new. He tells us this throughout Scripture. "Though your sins are like scarlet," God says, "they shall be like snow" (Isa. 1:18). Remember the woman who was unclean and hemorrhaging. She touched the Lord's garment and was made new (Mark 5:25–34). St. Mary Magdalene had seven demons cast out of her by coming into contact with the living God (Luke 8:2). And Jesus states in Revelation 21:3–6:

> And I heard a loud voice from the throne saying,
> "See, the home of God is among mortals.
> He will dwell with them;
> they will be his peoples,
> and God himself will be with them;
> he will wipe every tear from their eyes.
> Death will be no more;
> mourning and crying and pain will be no more,
> for the first things have passed away."
>
> And the one who was seated on the throne said, "See, I am making all things new." Also he said, "Write this, for these words are trustworthy and true." Then he said to me, "It is done! I am the Alpha and the Omega, the beginning and the end. To the thirsty I will give water as a gift from the spring of the water of life."

Let us allow God to make us new, to wipe away all our tears, and to restore us. We do this by the great blessing of prayer!

Prayer leads to sacrificial love: "In Christ Jesus neither circumcision nor uncircumcision counts for anything; the only thing that counts is faith working through love" (Gal. 5:6). We saw five ways to live out each devotion in honor of the five wounds of Christ. Now those ideas take on flesh in five groups of active works. In this way, the Mystical Body of Christ participates in carrying on the Incarnation of Christ in the world. Three of these groups of works console the heart of Christ (the Sacred Heart devotion), and two console the heart of man (the Divine Mercy devotion).

The first set of active works that console Jesus' heart are works of conversion. Heaven rejoices when a sinner returns to the Mystical Body of Christ: "There will be more joy in heaven over one sinner who repents than over ninety-nine righteous persons who need no repentance" (Luke 15:7). Works of conversion include visiting the homes of fallen-away Catholics, talking to people about God in a deep way, distributing Christian literature to those who have false ideas about God and religion, and seeking out the forsaken. The Lord told St. Faustina that even the gravest sinner would be embraced by His mercy if only they would come to the living waters.

The Legion of Mary handbook beautifully emphasizes this point:

> *Therefore, the work must proceed upon the principle of values reversed, that is, it shall concern itself especially with those whom even the optimist would term utterly hopeless cases, and whose warped minds and initial insensibility to appeal would seem to justify this description.* The vile, the malevolent, the naturally hateful, the rejects and black-listed of other societies and people, the refuse of cities, shall all be determinedly persevered with in spite of rebuffs, utter ingratitude, and apparent failure. Of these a considerable proportion will form a life-long task. *Obviously such a work, carried on according to such ideas, calls for heroic qualities and a purely supernatural vision. The compensation for toil so great will lie in the seeing of the objects of that toil eventually die in the friendship of God. Then what joy to have cooperated with "Him who from the mire, in patient length of days, Elaborated into life a people to His praise!"* (Bl. John Henry Newman: Dream of Gerontius).... In addition, it holds, amongst services done to the Church, a key position. *For it constitutes a special assertion of the Catholic principle that even the lowest of human beings hold in relation to us a position which is independent of their value or*

> *agreeableness to us: that in them Christ is to be seen, reverenced, loved.*[39] (emphasis mine)

We must be bold in approaching people that society deems "weird" or "not worth our time." Since Jesus died for all men, such people are worthy of hearing His gospel. After all, to say that someone is not worthy to hear the gospel is to take on the Jansenist mentality. We are not Jansenists; we are Christians! Thus, the Sacred Heart compels us to offer the gospel to all, especially the lost, the forsaken, and the greatest of sinners.

We also have a sacred duty to spread the Catholic Faith. St. Paul reminds us of this reality:

> "Everyone who calls on the name of the Lord shall be saved." *But how are they to call on one in whom they have not believed? And how are they to believe in one of whom they have never heard? And how are they to hear without someone to proclaim him? And how are they to proclaim him unless they are sent?* As it is written, "How beautiful are the feet of those who bring good news!" But not all have obeyed the good news; for Isaiah says, "Lord, who has believed our message?" So faith comes from what is heard, and what is heard comes through the word of Christ. (Rom. 10:13–17, emphasis mine)

Again, the Legion of Mary handbook offers a powerful perspective:

[39] Concilium Legionis Mariae, *The Official Handbook of the Legion of Mary* (Dublin, Ireland: De Monfort House, 2014), chap. 37, sec. 6, 240–241, https://www.legionofmary.ie/images/uploads/files/Official_Handbook_of_the_Legion_of_Mary_2014_-_as_updated_January_2022.pdf.

> The Church teaches them one world and they live in another. The voice of the secularized world speaks louder than that of the Church. *The imbalance must be corrected. The Christian's mandate is to win the secularized world for Christ. This demands that we have the right values and attitudes—the Christian ones.*[40] (emphasis mine)

So let us put our prayer into action by bringing to Christ's Sacred Heart those who do not know Him or who have strayed from Him. This could be the answer to someone's prayers.

The second way to activate prayer is through works of conservation. These are works that help people to maintain and grow their faith as well as their relationship with God. There are two ways we can do this to console the Sacred Heart. The first is to teach children the Faith. We know that Jesus loves children and says, "Let the little children come to me; do not stop them; for it is to such as these that the kingdom of God belongs" (Mark 10:14). It hurts Jesus' heart that some children do not love Him or even know about Him. Thus, we need to help children to learn what it means to be a Christian. It is not just a title we have or something we do; it is who we are. Regardless of our vocations, we must teach the four pillars of our Faith, found in the *Catechism*: the Creed, morality, the sacraments, and prayer. Jesus also says to everyone: "Truly I tell you, whoever does not receive the kingdom of God as a little child will never enter it" (Mark 10:15). So we adults, too, need to take time to study what we believe (the Creed), how to live it out (morality), how to get the power to live it out (through the sacraments), and how to nourish the *hesed covenantal* relationship we are all called to have with God (through prayer).

[40] Ibid., sec. 12, 252–253.

Another work of conservation is enthroning the Sacred Heart of Jesus and the Immaculate Heart of Mary in our homes. Fr. Patrick Peyton, the great promoter of the Rosary, would always say, "A family that prays together stays together." So too, a family that makes Jesus Christ the King of their household (and Mary the Queen) will console the heart of Jesus, strengthen their family bond, and obtain numerous graces in an abundant way. It delights God's heart when we remember Him and allow our houses to become little churches for His kingdom. Enthroning our homes also brings abundant blessings to our families, as Our Lord promised in His words to St. Margaret Mary, "I will bring peace to their homes" and "all who promote this devotion will have their names written on my heart." It consoles Jesus to have our names written, or signed, in His heart, just as He put His signature on the Divine Mercy image. In this, our trust in Jesus is written on our hearts.

The third group of works are to console Jesus' heart, and these include promoting Mass, Eucharistic Adoration, and activities and organizations that atone for sins against the Sacred Heart. Promoting Mass is essential as it calls to mind Jesus' sacrifice on Calvary re-presented (notice *not* represented) under sacramental signs. Presence shows appreciation, and appreciation brings consolation. This is the motivation for promoting Eucharistic Adoration. There is no greater honor than to be with the One who loves you, as we are in Adoration. As a devout peasant at St. John Vianney's parish described his time in front of the tabernacle, "I look at God and He looks at me" (see CCC 2715). Eucharistic Adoration is a pledge of love! This brings us to organizations that atone for sins against the Sacred Heart.

One such organization, mentioned earlier, is the Pioneer Total Abstinence Association of the Sacred Heart. This organization is made up of people who give up alcohol temporarily or permanently, not because it is bad in and of itself (after all, Jesus made more wine for the wedding at Cana [see John 2:1–12]) but to atone for the sins of intemperance pertaining to alcohol. These sins harm families, kill innocent people through drunk driving, and dehumanize people by making them lose their capacity to reason and make right judgments; these sins wound the Sacred Heart of Jesus. Hence, people in this association wear a Sacred Heart badge. The badge helps others see their sacrifice of alcohol, hopefully reminding others to be temperate and to console the Sacred Heart of Jesus. Members of the association say the following prayer twice a day:

> *For Your greater glory and consolation,*
> O *Sacred Heart of Jesus,*
> for your sake to give good example,
> to practise self-denial,
> *to make reparation for the sins of intemperance*
> *and for the conversion of excessive drinkers,*
> I will abstain for [the designated amount of time,
> such as "Lent" or "this month"] from all
> intoxicating drink. (emphasis mine)[41]

Jesus also wants to console human hearts. He provides His Mystical Body, the Church, to make sure that people know that He is walking with them and to embody His words "Do not let your hearts be troubled" (John 14:1).

First, there are works of consolation for the Mystical Body of Christ that help the Church to operate in a vibrant way. These

[41] "Heroic Offering to the Sacred Heart," Pioneer Total Abstinence Association of the Sacred Heart, https://www.pioneers.ie/pray.

include acts such as praying in Rosary groups, hosting the Pilgrim Virgin Statue to seek Mary's intercession for particular intentions, praying the Divine Mercy Chaplet at wakes and funerals to bring comfort to those who are grieving, and participating in pastoral visitation groups that keep people connected in the Church. The clergy cannot be everywhere, but the Church can and should be. It is the Church as a whole (both clergy and laypeople) who can offer meals for a family who just had a baby or experienced a death in the family. Various parishes have men's and women's groups so that each sex can help each other grow in holiness. Married couples can help with marriage preparation, so that young couples can have mentors to guide them and to show them that divorce is not the answer to difficulties in marriage. People often cry out to God, "What are You going to do about this situation?" God looks at each of us as members of the Church and says, "I did do something about it; I made you!" This is why comforting the sick, counseling the doubtful, instructing the ignorant, feeding the hungry, giving drink to the thirsty, clothing the naked, and even admonishing the sinner are works of mercy. We, as members of the Church, are called to "be merciful, just as your Father is merciful" (Luke 6:36) and bring His consolation to those who yearn for it.

This brings us to the second group of works that console man's heart: invitations to grace. Many souls want to know how to become better people, how to find fulfillment, how to deal with their problems, but they need an invitation to grace. Remember the man whom the disciples lowered through the roof so that Jesus could heal him:

> One day, while he was teaching, Pharisees and teachers of the law were sitting near by (they had come from every village of Galilee and Judea and from Jerusalem); and the power of the Lord was with him to heal. Just then some

> men came, carrying a paralyzed man on a bed. They were trying to bring him in and lay him before Jesus; but finding no way to bring him in because of the crowd, they went up on the roof and let him down with his bed through the tiles into the middle of the crowd in front of Jesus. When he saw their faith, he said, "Friend, your sins are forgiven you." Then the scribes and the Pharisees began to question, "Who is this who is speaking blasphemies? Who can forgive sins but God alone?" When Jesus perceived their questionings, he answered them, "Why do you raise such questions in your hearts? Which is easier, to say, 'Your sins are forgiven you,' or to say, 'Stand up and walk'? But so that you may know that the Son of Man has authority on earth to forgive sins"—he said to the one who was paralyzed—"I say to you, stand up and take your bed and go to your home." Immediately he stood up before them, took what he had been lying on, and went to his home, glorifying God. Amazement seized all of them, and they glorified God and were filled with awe, saying, "We have seen strange things today." (Luke 5:17–26)

Could Jesus have healed the paralytic without his being lowered through the roof? Yes, but Jesus wanted others to be His instruments in bringing the wounded man to the source of grace. It is the same with us. God wants us to cooperate and work with Him for the salvation of souls. St. Margaret Mary, the Apostle of the Sacred Heart, speaks a message of Divine Mercy when she says, "One just soul can attain pardon for a thousand sinners." *Apostle* means "one who is sent"; Jesus asks us all to be apostles of His mercy and His Sacred Heart. This will allow us to help those who are thirsty and who have no money to come to the water, as the prophet Isaiah reminds us:

> *All you who are thirsty,*
> *come to the water!*
> You who have no money,
> come, buy grain and eat;
> Come, buy grain without money,
> wine and milk without cost!
> (Isa. 55:1, NABRE, emphasis mine)

The living waters that flow from the heart of Christ are His Divine Mercy and love. He sends us out as apostles to bring people to the Sacred Heart, so they can be consoled by His Divine Mercy and so that He can be consoled by His Mystical Body fulfilling His mission and doing the Father's will to redeem the World. "For God so loved the world that he gave his only Son, so that everyone who believes in him may not perish but may have eternal life. Indeed, God did not send the Son into the world to condemn the world, but in order that the world might be saved through him" (John 3:16–17).

Conclusion

In this book, we have examined two of the most powerful devotions for our times: the Sacred Heart of Jesus and Divine Mercy devotions. We have seen their biblical roots, their history, and their historical context. Also, we have seen how God uses these devotions to blast heresies and poisonous sentiments that separate humanity from God and wound the hearts of God and man. These malicious heresies deny "the Father and the Son" (1 John 2:22). Since Jesus Christ, through His Incarnation, is both God and man, these attacks and poisons go against the Incarnation. They deny that "Jesus Christ has come in the flesh" (2 John 1:7). Thus, the Sacred Heart and Divine Mercy devotions are sure defenses against the antichrist. This is good news; we are not left defenseless against modernity. God truly does come to our assistance and hasten to help (see Ps. 69:2, Douay-Rheims; Ps. 70:5, NRSVCE).

Our focus must not be on simply what is wrong but must be directed toward what is good, true, and beautiful, as St. Paul tells us to "think about these things" (Phil. 4:8). God does not leave us hopeless and wallowing in our misery. He allows his hesed covenantal love to renew us, so that His love and our hearts always have the last word. As St. Margaret Mary Alacoque, the Apostle of the Sacred Heart, reminds us, "Look upon yourself as a tree planted beside the water, which bears its fruit in due season; the more it is shaken by the wind, the deeper it strikes its roots into the ground." An episode with St. Faustina, the Apostle of Divine Mercy, which we saw earlier, also demonstrates this beautifully:

> Jesus said to me, **"My daughter, you have not offered Me that which is really yours."** I probed deeply into myself and found that I love God with all the faculties of my soul and, unable to see what it was that I had not yet given to the Lord, I asked, "Jesus, tell me what it is, and I will give it to You at once with a generous heart." Jesus said to me with kindness, **"My Daughter, give Me your misery, because it is your exclusive property."** At that moment, a ray of light illumined my soul, and I saw the whole abyss of my misery. In that same moment I nestled close to the Most Sacred Heart of Jesus. (*Diary* 1318)

If we can help others to give all to Jesus Christ, then He can give His all to them and heal their wounds. This healing does not mean that things will "get back to normal," but it means that we are not alone. Jesus is with us, for "by his bruises we are healed" (Isa. 53:5).

Jesus holds nothing back from us. He became Incarnate for us, died for us on the Cross, given Himself to us in the Blessed Sacrament, and given us His transformative Word in Sacred Scripture. He walks with us in history through the Church and has given us the Sacred Heart and Divine Mercy devotions. He gives all, but we must open ourselves to be able to receive Him. We must allow ourselves to be consoled by His merciful heart and, in return, to console His heart through our "faith working through love" (Gal. 5:6). Let us bring God to people's hearts, for He alone offers hope. Hope will give them zeal in these trying times when so many feel "stuck." This zeal, combined with God's grace, manifested through His sacred and merciful heart, will once again make people fully alive. As St. Margaret Mary said, "Cling to God, and leave all the rest to Him: He will not let you perish. Your soul is very dear to Him, He wishes to save it." Pope Benedict XVI put it simply: "In hope we are saved" (Rom. 8:24).[42]

In this salvation, we will be renewed with a heavenly outlook because we will never have a bad day again. Let me explain. Mother Teresa would often say that crosses and sufferings were the kisses of Christ. These kisses mean that we are loved by Him and are united to Him in good times and in bad. If things are going well, we are being embraced with the joy that He has made us. We are being consoled by the Heart of Jesus Christ (the theme of the Divine Mercy devotion). If times are hard and God permits suffering, we are being kissed by Christ because He is asking us to offer up something for Him for the salvation of souls, "completing what is lacking in Christ's afflictions for the sake of his body, that is, the church" (Col. 1:24).

Suffering invites us to console Jesus' heart while He embraces us with His kiss (connecting to the Sacred Heart devotion). This embrace shows that Jesus is with us and we are with Him "in good times and in bad, in sickness and in health; that we will love and honor each other as long as we both shall live." These are the words of Catholic wedding vows, but they are just as much an icon of God's hesed love. This is the love worth living for and dying for. This is the love that the Sacred Heart and Divine Mercy devotions reveal. Let us embrace these wellsprings of grace so that we will stop living like the walking dead and instead live life abundantly (John 10:10). Jesus speaks to us in an inspiring way through the Sacred Heart and Divine Mercy devotions, and His message is summed up in the Gospel of John: "I have said these things to you so that

[42] Pope Benedict XVI, encyclical *Spe Salvi* (November 30, 2007).

my joy may be in you, and that your joy may be complete" (15:11). Let us embrace the Sacred Heart of Jesus and His Divine Mercy so that we can console God's heart. If we do, He will give us the grace to conquer every evil that plagues our world and ourselves, for His mercy endures forever.

Jesus meek and humble of heart,
make our hearts like unto Thine.

Jesus, I trust in You!

Appendix 1

Twelve Promises of the Sacred Heart

1. I will give them all the graces necessary in their state of life.
2. I will establish peace in their homes.
3. I will comfort them in all their afflictions.
4. I will be their secure refuge during life, and above all, in death.
5. I will bestow abundant blessings upon all their undertakings.
6. Sinners will find in my Heart the source and infinite ocean of mercy.
7. Lukewarm souls shall become fervent.
8. Fervent souls shall quickly mount to high perfection.
9. I will bless every place in which an image of my Heart is exposed and honored.
10. I will give to priests the gift of touching the most hardened hearts.
11. Those who shall promote this devotion shall have their names written in my Heart.
12. I promise you in the excessive mercy of my Heart that my all-powerful love will grant to all those who receive Holy

Communion on the First Fridays in nine consecutive months the grace of final perseverance; they shall not die in my disgrace, nor without receiving their sacraments. My divine Heart shall be their safe refuge in this last moment.[43]

[43] "12 Promises of the Sacred Heart to St. Margaret Mary Alacoque," EWTN, https://www.ewtn.com/catholicism/library/12-promises-of-the-sacred-heart-13683.

Appendix 2

How to Pray the Divine Mercy Chaplet

1. Make the Sign of the Cross.

   In the name of the Father, and of the Son, and of the Holy Spirit. Amen.

2. Optional Opening Prayers

   St. Faustina's Prayer for Sinners

   O Jesus, eternal Truth, our Life, I call upon You and I beg Your mercy for poor sinners. O sweetest Heart of my Lord, full of pity and unfathomable mercy, I plead with You for poor sinners. O Most Sacred Heart, Fount of Mercy from which gush forth rays of inconceivable graces upon the entire human race, I beg of You light for poor sinners. O Jesus, be mindful of Your own bitter Passion and do not permit the loss of souls redeemed at so dear a price of Your most precious Blood. O Jesus, when I consider the great price of Your Blood, I rejoice at its immensity, for one drop alone would have been enough for the salvation of all sinners.

Although sin is an abyss of wickedness and ingratitude, the price paid for us can never be equaled. Therefore, let every soul trust in the Passion of the Lord, and place its hope in His mercy. God will not deny His mercy to anyone. Heaven and earth may change, but God's mercy will never be exhausted. Oh, what immense joy burns in my heart when I contemplate Your incomprehensible goodness, O Jesus! I desire to bring all sinners to Your feet that they may glorify Your mercy throughout endless ages. (*Diary of Saint Maria Faustina Kowalska*, 72)

You expired, Jesus, but the source of life gushed forth for souls, and the ocean of mercy opened up for the whole world. O Fount of Life, unfathomable Divine Mercy, envelop the whole world and empty Yourself out upon us.

O Blood and Water, which gushed forth from the Heart of Jesus as a fount of mercy for us, I trust in You! (Repeat three times.)

3. Our Father

Our Father, Who art in heaven, hallowed be Thy name; Thy kingdom come; Thy will be done on earth as it is in heaven. Give us this day our daily bread; and forgive us our trespasses as we forgive those who trespass against us; and lead us not into temptation, but deliver us from evil, Amen.

4. Hail Mary

Hail Mary, full of grace. The Lord is with thee. Blessed art thou amongst women, and blessed is the fruit of thy womb, Jesus. Holy Mary, Mother of God, pray for us sinners, now and at the hour of our death. Amen.

5. The Apostles' Creed

I believe in God, the Father almighty, Creator of heaven and earth, and in Jesus Christ, His only Son, our Lord, who was conceived by the Holy Spirit, born of the Virgin Mary, suffered under Pontius Pilate, was crucified, died and was buried; He descended into hell; on the third day He rose again from the dead; He ascended into heaven, and is seated at the right hand of God the Father almighty; from there He will come to judge the living and the dead. I believe in the Holy Spirit, the holy catholic Church, the communion of saints, the forgiveness of sins, the resurrection of the body, and life everlasting. Amen.

6. The Eternal Father

Eternal Father, I offer you the Body and Blood, Soul and Divinity of Your Dearly Beloved Son, Our Lord, Jesus Christ, in atonement for our sins and those of the whole world.

7. On the 10 small beads of each decade

For the sake of His sorrowful Passion, have mercy on us and on the whole world.

8. Repeat for the remaining decades

Saying the "Eternal Father" (6) on the "Our Father" beads and then ten "For the sake of His sorrowful Passion" (7) on the following "Hail Mary" beads.

9. Conclude with Holy God (Repeat three times)

Holy God, Holy Mighty One, Holy Immortal One, have mercy on us and on the whole world.

10. Optional Closing Prayers

Eternal God, in whom mercy is endless and the treasury of compassion—inexhaustible, look kindly upon us and increase Your mercy in us, that in difficult moments we might not despair nor become despondent, but with great confidence submit ourselves to Your holy will, which is Love and Mercy itself.

O Greatly Merciful God, Infinite Goodness, today all mankind calls out from the abyss of its misery to Your mercy—to Your compassion, O God; and it is with its mighty voice of misery that it cries out. Gracious God, do

not reject the prayer of this earth's exiles! O Lord, Goodness beyond our understanding, Who are acquainted with our misery through and through, and know that by our own power we cannot ascend to You, we implore You: anticipate us with Your grace and keep on increasing Your mercy in us, that we may faithfully do Your holy will all through our life and at death's hour. Let the omnipotence of Your mercy shield us from the darts of our salvation's enemies, that we may with confidence, as Your children, await Your [Son's] final coming—that day known to You alone. And we expect to obtain everything promised us by Jesus in spite of all our wretchedness. For Jesus is our Hope: through His merciful Heart, as through an open gate, we pass through to heaven (*Diary* 1570).[44]

[44] "How To Recite the Chaplet," The Divine Mercy, https://www.thedivinemercy.org/message/devotions/pray-the-chaplet.

Bibliography

Aglialoro, Todd . "Jansenism." *Catholic Answers Magazine*, June 1, 1994. https://www.catholic.com/magazine/print-edition/jansenism.

Alar, Fr. Chris, M.I.C. *Understanding Divine Mercy*. Stockbridge, MA: Marian Press, 2021.

Anthony, Gerard-Marie. "Embracing Mary's Heart for Modernity." *Arlington Catholic Herald*, June 15, 2023. https://www.catholicherald.com/article/columns/embracing-marys-heart-for-modernity.

Aquinas, Thomas. *Summa Theologiae*. Translated by the Fathers of the English Dominican Province. 2nd rev. ed. 1920. New Advent. https://www.newadvent.org/summa/1.htm.

Benedict XVI. Encyclical letter *Spe Salvi*. November 30, 2007.

Burkepile, Jacqueline. "Visions of the Sacred Heart of Jesus: 4 Mystical Messages to St. Margaret Mary Alacoque." EWTN Great Britain. https://ewtn.co.uk/chpop-visions-of-the-sacred-heart-of-jesus-4-mystical-messages-to-st-margaret-mary-alacoque.

Concillium Legionis Mariae. *Official Handbook of the Legion of Mary*. Dublin: De Monfort House, 2014. https://www.legion

ofmary.ie/images/uploads/files/Official_Handbook_of_the_Legion_of_Mary_2014_-_as_updated_January_2022.pdf.

"Come, Holy Ghost." Hymnary.org. https://hymnary.org/text/come_holy_ghost_creator_blest.

Flynn, Dan. *Wheelbarrow: A Parable of Faith*. God Can. God Cares, May 26, 2020." https://godcangodcares.com/wheelbarrow-a-parable-of-faith.

"Fulton J. Sheen Quotes." AZ Quotes. https://www.azquotes.com/author/13447-Fulton_J_Sheen.

Gany, Alec. "Behold, This Heart That Loves So Much Yet Is So Little Loved." Clarifying Catholicism, October 18, 2019. https://clarifyingcatholicism.org/mariology-and-saints/behold-this-heart-that-loves-so-much-yet-is-so-little-loved.

"Heroic Offering to the Sacred Heart." Pioneer Total Abstinence Association of the Sacred Heart. https://www.pioneers.ie/pray.

John Paul II. Post-synodal apostolic exhortation *Ecclesia in America*. January 22, 1999.

Knight, Tim. "Chronos vs. Kairos." A Call to Excellence, February 27, 2023. https://www.acalltoexcellence.com/chronos-vs-kairos.

Kowalska, Faustina. *Divine Mercy in My Soul: Diary of Saint Maria Faustina Kowalska*. Stockbridge, MA: Marian Press, 2005.

Marian Fathers. "How to Recite the Chaplet." The Divine Mercy. https://www.thedivinemercy.org/message/devotions/pray-the-chaplet.

"Meaning of Numbers in the Bible: The Number 5." Bible Study. https://www.biblestudy.org/bibleref/meaning-of-numbers-in-bible/5.html.

"Mother Teresa." AZ Quotes. https://www.azquotes.com/quote/550653?ref=desolation.

Nault, Jean-Charles, O.S.B. *The Noonday Devil: Acedia, the Unnamed Evil of Our Times*. San Francisco: Ignatius Press, 2013.

O'Donnell, Timothy. *Heart of the Redeemer: An Apologia for the Contemporary and Perennial Value of the Devotion to the Sacred Heart of Jesus*. San Francisco: Ignatius Press, 1992.

Pius IX. *The Syllabus of Errors*. December 8, 1864. Papal Encyclicals. https://www.papalencyclicals.net/pius09/p9syll.htm.

Pius X. Encylical *Pascendi Dominici Gregis*. September 8, 1907.

Pius XI. Encyclical *Divini Redemptoris*. March 19, 1937.

"Quotes by Mother Teresa—Poverty." All Saints and Martyrs, November 26, 2018. https://saintscatholic.blogspot.com/2018/11/quotes-by-mother-teresa-poverty.html.

Sacred Heart Apostolate. "12 Promises of the Sacred Heart." In *Why Do I Need to Enthrone an Image of the Sacred Heart of Jesus in My Home?* Sacred Heart Apostolate. https://sacredheartapostolate.com/wp-content/uploads/2018/07/Why-Enthrone-An-Image-of-the-Sacred-Heart-trifold.pdf.

Saunders, Fr. William. "What Is the Role of Novenas Today?" EWTN, August 25, 1994. https://www.ewtn.com/catholicism/library/what-is-the-role-of-novenas-today-1098.

Sisters of the Visitation of Paray-le- Monial, The. *Thoughts and Sayings of Saint Margaret Mary*. Rockford, IL: TAN Books and Publishing, 1986.

"St. John Eudes." The Eudists. https://www.eudistsusa.org/st-john-eudes.

Stackpole, Robert. "On Going to Confession before Mercy Sunday." The Divine Mercy, March 28, 2007. https://www.thedivinemercy.org/articles/going-confession-mercy-sunday.

"12 Promises of the Sacred Heart to St. Margaret Mary Alacoque." EWTN. https://www.ewtn.com/catholicism/library/12-promises-of-the-sacred-heart-13683.

Vazhakala, Fr. Sebastian. *The M.C. Tree*. Pittsburgh: Dorrance Publishing, 2020.

About the Author

Deacon Gerard-Marie Anthony is an avid promotor of the Sacred Heart and Divine Mercy devotions. He does this as a scholar lecturer for Sophia Institute for Teachers and professor at the Virginia Catholic Biblical School, headed by Dr. Nicholas Lebish. He has five big apostolates that embody these devotions: Mother of Light Center (https://www.motheroflightcenter.com), which helps give the love of God and dignity to those experiencing material and spiritual poverty in life; A Mom's Peace (https://www.amomspeace.org), which helps mothers and families who have experienced miscarriage or stillbirths; the Associates of St. John Bosco (https://www.asjb.org), which help high schoolers transition and keep their faith in college and trains young adults in the apostolate; the Legion of Mary (https://www.legionofmary.ie), which is the world's biggest organization for evangelization; and Divine Mercy Home (https://divinemercyhome.org), which helps give dignity to those experiencing end-of-life issues.

Sophia Institute

Sophia Institute is a nonprofit institution that seeks to nurture the spiritual, moral, and cultural life of souls and to spread the gospel of Christ in conformity with the authentic teachings of the Roman Catholic Church.

Sophia Institute Press fulfills this mission by offering translations, reprints, and new publications that afford readers a rich source of the enduring wisdom of mankind.

Sophia Institute also operates the popular online resource CatholicExchange.com. *Catholic Exchange* provides world news from a Catholic perspective as well as daily devotionals and articles that will help readers to grow in holiness and live a life consistent with the teachings of the Church.

In 2013, Sophia Institute launched Sophia Institute for Teachers to renew and rebuild Catholic culture through service to Catholic education. With the goal of nurturing the spiritual, moral, and cultural life of souls, and an abiding respect for the role and work of teachers, we strive to provide materials and programs that are at once enlightening to the mind and ennobling to the heart; faithful and complete, as well as useful and practical.

Sophia Institute gratefully recognizes the Solidarity Association for preserving and encouraging the growth of our apostolate over the course of many years. Without their generous and timely support, this book would not be in your hands.

www.SophiaInstitute.com
www.CatholicExchange.com
www.SophiaInstituteforTeachers.org